c/P

THE
ENGLISH TRADITION
IN DESIGN

BY

JOHN GLOAG

ADAM & CHARLES BLACK
LONDON

First published as a King Penguin Book, 1947

New, enlarged and revised edition
published 1959 by A. & C. Black Ltd.
4, 5 & 6 Soho Square, London, W.1

PRINTED IN GREAT BRITAIN
in 11-*point Baskerville type*
BY UNWIN BROTHERS LIMITED
WOKING AND LONDON

CONTENTS

ILLUSTRATIONS IN THE TEXT

LIST OF PLATES

MEDIAEVAL ROOTS

WILLIAM COBBETT'S *History of the Protestant Reformation* started a fashion for depicting in variously fanciful ways the civilisation of mediaeval England. Some of the pictures are tenderly romantic, like *A Dream of John Ball* and *The Story of the Unknown Church* by William Morris; others are charged with the boisterous energy that explodes in the first four lines of Chesterton's poem, *The Englishman*:

> St. George he was for England,
> And before he killed the dragon
> He drank a pint of English ale
> Out of an English flagon.

The down-to-earth, practical heartiness of that sentiment is certainly reflected in line after line of *The Canterbury Tales;* and the things that were built and made and used in the thirteenth, fourteenth and fifteenth centuries suggest that the mediaeval Englishman, and in particular the craftsman, was well equipped with common sense and a capacity for enjoying such good things as life then offered. Mason, smith and joiner handled their materials with a familiarity that bred neither contempt nor a lordly and arrogant sense of power, but love and respect: they wore their mastery of wood and metal and stone very lightly: they coaxed materials and never bullied them, nor were they ever discouraged by their obduracy—they accepted it as a challenge to invention. Those men were slowly establishing a tradition of design, broadening and deepening skills which had been handed on generation after generation, from the days of that vivid, short-lived and accomplished civilisation in Northumbria—when Bede could write of "the peaceable and calm disposition of the times"— through the shadows of Danish raids and Saxon disunity, until

The Foundress' Cup, at Christ's College, Cambridge, *circa* 1440. The diagonal bands of foliated ornament are in repoussé and Gothic cresting encircles the cover and the base. Cripps states that "the arms enamelled on the boss within the cup are those of Humphrey, Duke of Gloucester, impaled with Cobham of Sternborough, and this impalement, being the distinctive coat of Duke Humphrey's second wife Eleanor Cobham according to the heraldry of that day, would point to 1440, or a year or two earlier, as the true date of the cup." From *Old English Plate*, by Wilfred Joseph Cripps, reproduced by permission of the publishers, John Murray, and of Christ's College, Cambridge.

the Norman Conquest unified the country and Norman builders unified and expanded the crafts. Thus tutored for nearly four hundred years by the Mistress Art, English craftsmen had, by the end of the fifteenth century, created a recognisable style in woodwork and, to a lesser extent, in metalwork. In stained glass and stone carving, illuminated manuscripts, goldsmith's work and embroidery, English achievements were famous; but it is in woodwork that the national and characteristic approach to design has most clearly persisted. From the time when the joined chests of the thirteenth and fourteenth centuries were decorated with roundels of chip carving to the masterly cabinet-making of such latter-day artist-craftsmen as Ernest Gimson and Sidney Barnsley, Ambrose Heal and Gordon Russell, an unmistakable affinity of purpose is apparent, disclosing an affectionate sympathy for materials, a sense of apt selection and gay orderliness in the forms of embellishment, which are inseparable ingredients of the English tradition in design.

The proper study of that tradition is to follow its manifestations in the things that were built and made. They have something to say, not only of national character, but of local materials, ideas and habits; they can be as expressive and recognisable as local dialects—as unmistakable as broad Yorkshire or the accents of Lancashire, Somerset, Gloucester, Norfolk and Devon. "The localness of English art," said John Sedding, "is one of its distinguishing marks—a mark that the text books cannot enforce. How can the text books be at once general and local, comprehensive and particular, generic and specific? Study the art locally, for that is how it grew: its initiation was mostly with the horny-handed workman, so far, at least, as details are concerned; its

Oak framed chest, with the front decorated with chip-carved roundels, and the inner side of the feet worked into small shafts. From Stoke d'Abernon Church, Surrey. *Circa* 1300. From Parker's *Glossary*, Oxford, 1845.

Doorway at Merton College Chapel, Oxford, *circa* 1424. An early example of the culminating achievement of English Gothic architecture — the Perpendicular style. From Parker's *Glossary*, Oxford, 1845. See pages 8 and 9.

foster mother was tradition; its cradle was the tradesman's bench. The patron might scheme the building, look on and direct the work, but he did not invent the details; indeed, you can scarcely say that anything was 'original' in those days; so related was everything to what had gone before, and what was going on elsewhere."[1]

Even before the beginning of the Tudor period, a native English style had emerged, and was apparent in Royal, ecclesiastical and domestic architecture and the ancillary arts and crafts. It represented a splendid partnership of slender stonework, coloured glass, warm-hued brickwork and decorative plaster, wood acting sturdily as the structural framework, or clothing walls with carved panelling, or providing stout and serviceable but never clumsy tables and benches and chairs, though the latter were rare and used only for state occasions. Joiner, turner and carver worked in collaboration, nor were their activities segregated until the fourth decade of the seventeenth century.

[1] "On the Study of English Architecture," a paper read by John D. Sedding to the Sheffield Architectural Society, and included in his collected papers and essays, published under the title of *Art and Handicraft*. (London: Kegan Paul, Trench, Trubner & Co. Ltd., 1893.) Pages 15–16.

Pew ends with blind tracery, *circa* 1500, showing the relationship to Perpendicular Gothic forms. *Left:* Steeple Aston. *Right:* Great Tew. Oxfordshire. From Parker's *Glossary*, Oxford 1845.

Stools and chairs with turned spindles were made during the Middle Ages, and the Turners Guild was known to have existed early in the fourteenth century, though it was probably far older. (It was granted a charter of incorporation as a City Company in 1604.) Those craftsmen used oak, of which John Evelyn wrote: "The *Land* and the *Sea* do sufficiently speak for the improvement of this excellent material; *Houses*, and *Ships*, *Cities*, and *Navies* are built with it; and there is a *kind* of it so *tough*, and extreamly compact, that our sharpest *Tools* will hardly enter it, and scarcely the very *Fire* itself, in which it consumes but slowly, as seeming to partake of a *ferruginous*, and *metallin* shining nature, proper for sundry robust Uses."[1] Oak might be as hard as iron, but its staunch quality commended it to woodworkers, who used it for the framing of houses, the panelling of walls and the furnishing of

[1] *Sylva, or a Discourse of Forest-Trees and the Propagation of Timber in His Majesties Dominions*, by John Evelyn. (London: Printed for John Martyn. Third edition, 1679.) Chapter III, page 25.

Mid-fifteenth century oak seat in St. Mary's Hall, Coventry: probably the right-hand part of a triple seat, which occupied the dais of the Great Hall, built in the early part of the century for the united guilds of St. Mary, St. John the Baptist and St. Catherine. Like the pew ends on page 5, the design reflects the characteristic ornament of contemporary Gothic architecture. (See page opposite.)

Back view of the oak seat shown opposite. Both drawings are reproduced from *Furniture with Candelabra and Interior Decoration*, by Richard Bridgens. London: 1838.

rooms, and carvers were not intimidated by its resistant surface. Their ornamental devices flowed along beams and enlivened panels with geometric and naturalistic motifs, of which the linenfold pattern and the convolutions of the vine became the most familiar. Doors and panels and the fronts of chests would sometimes display in miniature the structural and decorative forms of Perpendicular Gothic architecture, with surfaces resembling blind windows, filled with intricate tracery and giving to wooden chests or silver caskets the likeness of some shrine seen, as it were, through the wrong end of a telescope.

B

The tower of St. Mary Magdalene, at Taunton, Somerset. Late fifteenth century. *From a drawing by F. T. Dollman, made about* 1840.

The final phase of English Gothic architecture, the Perpendicular style, derived its name from the emphatic verticality of its lines—its slender window tracery and interior and exterior decoration. It arose late in the fourteenth century and flourished until the early years of the sixteenth, when it was modified during the Tudor period. The interior of Henry VII's Chapel (1502–15) in Westminster Abbey is one of the last and finest examples of Perpendicular Gothic. *Drawn by A. S. Cook.*

The Clock Tower in the Clock Court at Cardinal Wolsey's Palace at Hampton (1515–1530), showing the steps on the right inside the archway, which lead to the Great Hall (see page 11). A fine example of the native English style in domestic architecture which preserved in windows and interior decoration the characteristics of Perpendicular Gothic, apparent here and in such great houses as Compton Wynyates (see page 13). *Drawn by A. S. Cook.*

The Great Hall at Hampton Court Palace, built by Henry VIII after the death of Cardinal Wolsey, and occupying the north side of the Clock Court (see page 10). In this view, part of the hammer-beam roof is shown, also the tall window, and the original dais. The walls are hung with tapestry, and the windows glow with coloured heraldic devices. *Drawn by A. S. Cook.*

The sixteenth century, which was one of social and economic change, opened with the arts and crafts of England in a condition of felicitous stability; when colour entered into life with a natural vigour that was subsequently forgotten, and the selection and arrangement of representations of the foliage and flowers of English trees and gardens, and the beasts of the field and the chase, were carried out with an innate sense of decorative fitness that never overburdened any surface or subdued the gaiety and vitality of the designer's conception, whether it was expressed in terms of wood or precious metal, tapestry or painted plaster.

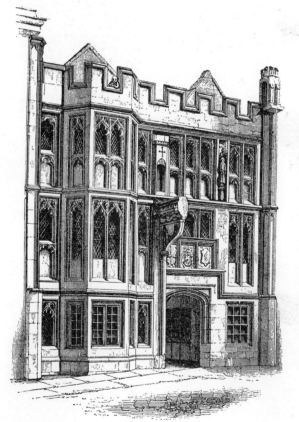

The George Inn, Glastonbury, originally built by Abbot John Selwood about 1480, as a hostelry for pilgrims. An example of the native English style which developed in the late fifteenth and early sixteenth centuries. From a drawing by William Twopeny, included in Parker's *Domestic Architecture in England*, Oxford, 1859.

Compton Wynyates, Warwickshire, 1520, completed by Sir William Compton, a London merchant. This shows the tall bay window in the court, and the comfortable association of brickwork and stone. From Parker's *Domestic Architecture in England*.

National talent for design had attained fluency and coherence: liberated from the almost exclusive patronage of the Church, architects and craftsmen were ready for fresh adventures and experiments in the building and furnishing of the great country houses and palaces desired by the new rich class that arose and flourished under the Tudor monarchs. But the opportunity was soon severely qualified by imported fashions, and the development of the English tradition in design became confused and partly arrested for over a century.

The tower of St. Michael, Huyton, Lancashire, which crowns a hill and is a
conspicuous landmark over a wide stretch of country. The tower has eight
stone pinnacles, surmounted by gilded metal wind-vanes in the form of pierced
banners. The upper part of the tower is an example of the native tradition of
building persisting far into the seventeenth century, for the date 1664 is
inscribed on the top. Over a hundred years earlier, in 1555, the church was
in a ruinous condition, and repairs were carried out in the sixteenth and
seventeenth centuries. No attempt was made to introduce classical features.
Drawn by David Owen.

2

FIRST INTERRUPTION BY FASHION

W**HEN** members of the new nobility took to travelling abroad and bringing back foreign ideas about shapes, colours, decoration and morals, popular resentment at such innovations was expressed by this rhyme:

> The Englishman Italianate
> Is the Devil incarnate.

The fashion for sending the sons of the nobility and gentry to Italy was criticised by William Harrison, who observed that they brought back "nothing but meere atheisme, infidelite, vicious conversation, & ambitious and proud behaviour, whereby it commeth to passe that they returne far worsse men than they went out."[1] But it was their exotic and extravagant taste that perplexed English craftsmen who had to satisfy the demands of their wealthy customers. The new rich are always a disruptive influence in the history of design, unless they are intimidated by established taste and are still in the humble, imitative stage of social development. The mercantile aristocracy that rose to power in the reign of Henry VIII was anything but humble: arrogant, acquisitive and supremely confident, the best was good enough for them, and in matters of taste, the best, they believed, came from Italy.

It was no new thing for some foreign influence to affect the work of English craftsmen; but previously such influences had been absorbed and understood; they emanated from fellow craftsmen in countries that were in a parallel phase of civilisation—the phase that had made the conception of united Christen-

---

[1] *Harrison's Description of England*, edited by Frederick J. Furnivall. (London: published for the New Shakespere Society by N. Trubner, 1877.) Part I, Book II, Chapter V, page 129.

dom a spiritual reality, and had inspired the Gothic architecture of North-Western Europe. French and Flemish ideas had been comfortably accommodated; but the "Italianate" fashions of the mid-sixteenth century were wholly different; intellectually and artistically alien, they represented a new mode of thought, a new approach to life; and in England it was perceived that the fashions were not unrelated to the new values and moral codes of the people who introduced them. It was a period not only of social and economic change but of intellectual ferment. Professor Macneile Dixon has pointed out that "Side by side with men conspicuous for genius and accomplishments, it threw up men conspicuous for wickedness, men at their best in every department of taste, and at their worst in every department of conduct."[1]

Those much-travelled noblemen wished to introduce the classic orders of architecture that had been standardised in the Roman Empire and revived by the architects of the Italian Renaissance, who used them with a freedom and significance transcending anything Roman. But in England classic architecture was not then recognised as an illuminating system of design, a regulating framework for the proportions and embellishment of almost everything that was made. It was regarded merely as a fashion and resented as such by craftsmen who had to conform to its apparent requirements in their work: so they borrowed and misinterpreted its external features, applying them to the sturdy basic shapes that had been evolved in the native English tradition. They derived their ideas of the Roman orders and their characteristic ornament from copy books, like the *Architectura* of Vredeman de Vries, issued in 1563 at Antwerp, and his *Compartimenta*, published three years later. These and other Flemish pattern books, with their copious use of strapwork, had a marked effect on the ideas of English builders and woodworkers. The new houses that were designed to accommodate these heady foreign fashions lacked the sturdy simplicity of the native style and were as unacceptable to that discerning and outspoken Englishman, William Harrison, as foreign manners and morals. "And albeit that in these daies there be manie goodlie houses erected in the sundrie

[1] *The Englishman*, by W. Macneile Dixon (Edward Arnold & Co. 1931.) Chapter IV, page 151.

The use of traditional materials preserved for centuries the characteristics of the pre-Elizabethan, native English style: timber framing, weather-boarding for walls, thatch and tiles for roofs were used for such structures as barns, throughout large areas of England, and for cottages and farm houses too. This example, near Deptford in Kent, was drawn and engraved by J. T. Smith in 1797. (See page 14.)

quarters of this Island," he wrote, "yet they are rather curious to the eie [like paper worke,] than substantiall for continuance...."[1]

As that form of surface decoration known as strapwork consisted of interlacing bands and scrolls, variegated with shields, shells, cartouches and lozenge and diamond shaped patches, Harrison's reference to "paper worke" may have been prompted by its fanciful convolutions, which looked as if they had been cut out of paper; but he may instead have been thinking of the increased slenderness suggested by the tall, generous bay windows which,

[1] *Harrison's Description of England*, edited by Frederick J. Furnivall. Part I, Book II, Chapter XV, page 268.

The Chapman Cup, at Armourers'
Hall, London, *circa* 1580. The
cover was added to the cup in
1610. The cup was presented
to the Company in 1581 by
Edmond Chapman. The effect of
Flemish interpretations of classical ornament is marked in the
decoration of this cup. The belt
of foliage round the upper part
lacks the freedom and vigour that
characterises the use of naturalistic motifs on the Reade Salt,
shown on plate 8, or the accomplished composition of the fire dog
from Haddon Hall on the opposite
page. The whole design illustrates
the "artistic incertitudes and experimental fumbling with unfamiliar, formalised ornament"
characteristic of an age of transition, when the native English
style was giving place to Italianate
fashions. From *Old English Plate*,
by Wilfred Joseph Cripps, reproduced by permission of the
publishers, John Murray, and The
Armourers and Brasiers' Company.

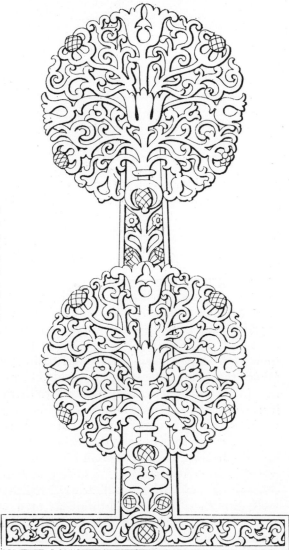

One of a pair of fire dogs from Haddon Hall, Derbyshire. A bold, orderly use of formalised naturalistic motifs that owe little to classical conventions of ornament, but are influenced by the Flemish pattern books that were popular in the late sixteenth century. *After Bridgens*.

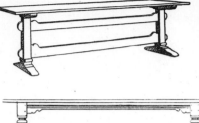

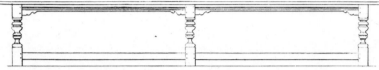

Left: Early sixteenth-century trestle table. *Drawn by Ronald Escott. Below:* Long table from Penshurst Place, Kent, with turned legs: a late sixteenth or early seventeenth-century design that is unaffected by classical ornament. *After Bridgens.*

ascending through two or more stories, appeared flimsy to the eyes of a traditionalist, for the new styles were just as shocking to conservative minds then as the new Western architecture is today, with its frank, uninhibited use of contemporary materials and constructional techniques. Harrison's *Description of England* was written before Hardwick Hall, in Derbyshire, was built; but its projecting bays, that are virtually glazed towers, and the great expanse of glass which dominates the façade, would have seemed as repellent to a lover of the discarded native style as the glass curtain walling of a contemporary building seems to a lover of Georgian architecture, whose affection for familiar forms debars him from appreciating the new architectural graces that are arising throughout the Western world. The inability to understand new ideas, which generates resistance to them, is as old as humanity: the innovating, uncommon man who launches some new idea or attempts to popularise a novel fashion or propagates a new way of thought has to overcome the inertia or active hostility of ordinary people, for the common man is so often what H. G. Wells once called "the common fool." The Elizabethan craftsmen who resisted the new fashions of the early English renaissance were not fools, but they were as obstinate as men who are set in their ways are apt to be, and this showed in their work. Acanthus leaves, scrolls, rosettes, corpulent versions of Ionic and Corinthian columns and pilasters, and the figures of classical gods and heroes were carved bluntly, and with small respect or sympathy, by men whose grandfathers had brought to the decoration of

English Gothic buildings a sensitive delicacy of touch and had endowed with spiritual emotion the sculptured figures of saints and angels.

Art had become a specialised, aristocratic study; the craftsman who was also the designer in the Middle Ages was becoming the artisan, the workman whose skilled hands obeyed directions dictated by fashionable taste. He was losing his independence and and his right to initiate ideas. It was the first rift between art and life since the barbarian invasions of the fifth and sixth centuries had destroyed the Roman province of Britain. Another and wider rift occurred after the First Industrial Revolution and the taste of the new rich, mercantile classes of the late sixteenth and early seventeen centuries anticipated the coarse lavishness we associate with the Victorian period. The Elizabethan age, like the Victorian, produced great literature and poetry and was a time of expansion

Mid-seventeenth-century improvements in furniture design.

Double gate-leg table with spiral twist on legs.

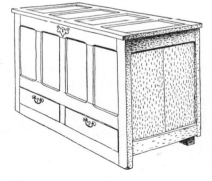

Above: Chair table. *Right:* Mule chest. *Drawn by Ronald Escott.*

and adventure and sublime confidence in the rectitude of current ideas, but design was in eclipse, while the printing and circulation of copy books purporting to give details and instructions about the use of the classsic orders of architecture did little to lighten the darkness, although the first English work on the subject was a straightforward guide without the fancifulness of the Flemish publications. It was issued by John Shute in 1563 and entitled *The First and Chief Groundes of Architecture*: later editions appeared in 1579, 1584 and 1587. Meanwhile craftsmen struggled on, resentfully confused, while their patrons, the great lords and merchant princes and the gay, glittering gentlemen that adorned Queen Elizabeth's court and played with equal ability the parts of lover, poet, soldier, or trading, fighting, exploring mariner, were intoxicated with the ideas that flowed into England from East and West. From Europe came the classic orders and the system of design they represented, with French and Spanish as well as Flemish versions of the original Italian interpretations; from the New World came a sultry intensity of colour, that introduced an almost tropical exuberance to the interior decoration and furnishing of houses. It was the last time that colour so vividly affected everyday surroundings, and the memory of it was almost effaced within half a century by the calculated austerity of the Puritan period, when England became for a few years a bleakly efficient, unhappy republic and, as Oliver Cromwell put it, people had to have "Not what they want but what is good for them."

The Elizabethan period was an age of transition, of artistic incertitudes and experimental fumbling with unfamiliar, formalised ornament. There were a few elegant trifles; some delicate and well-proportioned domestic glass; but goldsmiths and silversmiths were as confused as woodworkers, and cups and plates and caskets were often overloaded with ill-conceived classic motifs. (An exception is the Reade Salt, shown on plate 8.) Some of the more ambitious examples of Elizabethan silver might pass for exhibits at the Great Exhibition of 1851, though things of common use, such as pewter vessels and latten and brass candlesticks, were uncomplicated by concessions to fashion. They were shaped with the masterly competence that was still exercised in rural districts, too remote to be influenced by modish notions, for

Examples of decoration, depending on surface variations, invented and perfected by craftsmen, working in the native tradition, and uninfluenced by classical motifs. (See plates 1, 2 and 4.)

Left: Cut and moulded brickwork from Thornbury Castle, Gloucestershire, *circa* 1514. From Parker's *Glossary.*

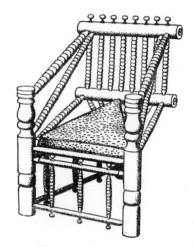

Above: Turned chair of East Anglian origin, *circa* 1600. In the Fitzwilliam Museum, Cambridge. *Drawn by Ronald Escott.*

Above: Gouge carving, used on flat surfaces in the late sixteenth century.

Right: Bobbin and spiral turning, which developed after the middle years of the seventeenth century. (See plates 10 and 11.) *Drawn by Ronald Escott.*

C

in the countryside the English tradition of design remained undisturbed for centuries. An example may be seen on the upper part of the tower of Huyton parish church in Lancashire, which was rebuilt in the late Gothic style after the Restoration of Charles II, and bears the date 1664. (See page 14.) As late as the 1920's there were a few "lost" pockets of mediaeval art in the west of England, notably in the Cotswolds, where masons and joiners still shaped stone and wood as they had been shaped by craftsmen four hundred years earlier, doing so unconsciously, for their little family businesses, enjoying unbroken continuity with the past, had worked in the same way generation after generation without guidance from professional architects.

During the sixteenth century the production and use of textiles greatly increased. Cushions, bed curtains and small hangings on walls behind benches, called dorcers or dorsals, as well as great tapestries covering walls from ceiling to floor, had been used in furnishing mediaeval palaces, and great houses; and the variety and scale of such luxuries are suggested by the description of the apartments prepared for the reception of a French noble-man who was entertained by Edward IV in 1472. This account occurs in a late fifteenth-century document entitled "The Co'minge into Englande of the Lorde Grautehuse from the Right high' and myghty Prince Charles Duke of Burgoine," and reads as follows:

Then, aboute ix of the clocke, the Kinge and quene, w^t her ladies and gentlewomen, brought the sayde Lorde Grautehuse to iij chaumbres of Pleasance, alt hanged w^t whyte Sylke and lynnen clothe, and alt the Floures couered w^t carpettes. There was ordeined a Bedde for hym selue, of as good doune as coulde be gotten, the Shetes of Raynys, also fyne Fustyans; the Counter-

Arcaded panels, on the front of a chest. Early seventeenth century.

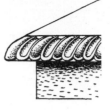

Decoration depending on
surface variations.

Above right: Gadrooning or nulling, a form of
carved fluting, with alternate concave and convex
flutes. *Left:* Mid-seventeenth-century chair with
arched back rails, carved with scrolls, and with
split turned balusters on the vertical members of
the back. A combination of the work of joiner,
turner, and carver. *Drawn by Ronald Escott.*

poynte clothe of golde, furred w[t] armyn, the Tester and the Celer
also shyninge clothe of golde, the Curteyns of whyte Sarsenette;
as for his hedde Sute and Pillowes, [they] were of the quenes
owen Ordonnance. Itm̃, [in] the ij[de] chambre was a other of
astate, the whiche was alte whyte. Also in the same chambre was
made a couche w[t] Fether beddes, hanged w[t] a Tente, knytt lyke
a nette, and there was a Cuppborde. Itm̃, in the iij[de] chambre
was ordeined a Bayne or ij, which were couered w[t] Tentes of
white clothe. And when the Kinge and the quene, w[t] alt her
ladyes and gentlewemen, had shewed him these chambres, they
turned againe to theire owen chambres, and lefte the sayde lorde
Grautehuse there, accompanied w[t] my lorde chamberlein, whiche
dispoyled hym, and wente both together to the Bayne [bath].[1]

A tester or teaster was a flat canopy over a chair of state, a
pulpit, or a bed: a celer, variously known as a celure, selour or
sellore, was the panel at the head of a bed; and celer and tester,
as in the description just quoted, were usually of the same material,
the former often being ornamented with the arms of the owner.

The demand for fabrics, for wall hangings and for bed curtains,
expanded during the Elizabethan period, though only a few,

[1] *Archaeologia*, Vol. XXVI, Section IX, pages 279–80, "Narratives of the arrival of
Louis de Bruges, Seigneur de la Gruthuyse, in England, and of his creation as Earl of
Winchester, in 1472." This includes a copy of a document MS. Add. 6113, f. 103,
in which this description of the bedroom furnishing occurs.

Exterior of the Presbyterian Meeting House, Cranbrook, Kent, as it appeared in the early nineteenth century. The upper storey is faced with weather-boards—or clap-boards as they were called in America—overlapping each other like courses of tiles. The windows are of the type used in the sixteenth and seventeenth centuries, with casements, before the sliding sash was generally adopted.

tentative experiments were made in upholstery: loose cushions on stools, benches and chairs were usual, and while chairs with X-shaped frames were covered with fabric or leather and garnished with nails, such types were coffer-makers' chairs, being the work of those particular craftsmen who were expert in covering wooden trunks and coffers with leather.[1] They depended for comfort on a loose cushion: there was as yet no close association of wooden framework, padding and covering material. Meanwhile the variety and output of woven fabrics expanded, and after the middle of the sixteenth century foreign weavers settled in England, in Kent and Essex, and around Norwich in Norfolk.

[1] "The Craft of the Coffer-Maker," by R. W. Symonds. *The Connoisseur*, Volume CVII, January–June, 1941, page 100.

Early in the 1560's William Sheldon, a Warwickshire squire, established a tapestry-weaving works at his manor house of Barcheston, under the direction of Richard Hyckes, who had studied the art in the Low Countries. Wall hangings, and large tapestry maps of English counties, as well as smaller woven pieces for cushion covers were made at the Sheldon manufactory. The colours have faded now, but when those hangings and cushion covers were new, they must have blazed on walls and seats, their hues occasionally intensified as some shaft of sunlight fell on them, tinted ruby or cerulean by its passage through a roundel of stained glass set high in a window or frieze light. In the composition and design of those great woven pictures and decorative pieces, heraldic and naturalistic motifs were handled with confidence, and Biblical and classical scenes depicted with spirit, for

Early seventeenth-century houses, behind the Charterhouse, London, as they appeared at the end of the eighteenth century, with irregular fenestration, and an air of haphazard growth rather than considered design. Architecturally they are far inferior to the purposeful orderliness of the native English style of the early Tudor period. From *The European Magazine*, February, 1797.

the English tradition was still unfettered in this field, and flowers, fruit, foliage and geometrical patterns were used without any reference to the prevailing Italianate taste (see plate 5). Wood-workers no longer enjoyed such freedoms, and in the houses of wealthy people, the huge carved beds, standing four square like malformed Roman temples, betrayed more emphatically than any other article their makers' profound ignorance of the rules that governed the proportions of the classic orders of architecture.

The richness of furnishing in all classes of homes is recorded by William Harrison, who observed that in the houses of noblemen it was "not rare to see abundance of Arras, rich hangings of tapistrie, silver vessell, and so much other plate, as may furnish sundrie cupboards, to the summe oftentimes of a thousand or two thousand pounds at the least: whereby the value of this and the rest of their stuffe dooth grow to be [almost] inestimable. Likewise in the houses of knights, gentlemen, merchantmen, and some other wealthie citizens, it is not geson to behold generallie their great profusion of tapistrie, Turkie worke, pewter, brasse, fine linen, and thereto costlie cupboards of plate, worth five or six hundred [or a thousand] pounds, to be deemed by estimation. But as herein all these sorts doo far exceed their elders and predecessors, [and in neatness and curiositie, the merchant all other;] so in time past, the costlie furniture staied there, whereas now it is descended yet lower, even unto the inferiour artificiers and manie farmers who [by vertue of their old and not of their new leases] have [for the most part] learned also to garnish their cupboards with plate, their [joined] beds with tapistrie and silk hangings, and their tables with [carpets &] fine naperie, whereby the wealth of our countrie [[(God be praised therefore, and give us grace to imploie it well)] dooth infinitelie appeare."[1]

When the Dutch physician, Levinus Lemnius, visited England in 1560 he was enchanted with the English character and the English home. In praising the latter he said, "the neate cleanliness, the exquisite finenesse, the pleasaunte and delightfull furniture in every poynt for household, wonderfully rejoysed mee; their chambers and parlours strawed over with sweete herbes refreshed mee; their nosegayes finely entermingled wyth sundry sortes of

---

[1] *Harrison's Description of England*, edited by Frederick J. Furnivall. Part I, Book II, Chapter XII, pages 238–9.

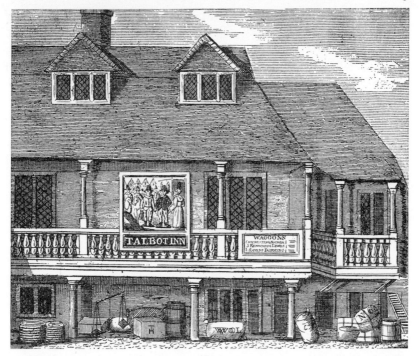

The Talbot Inn, in Borough High Street, Southwark, which was known as
the Tabard until the end of the sixteenth century: it was largely rebuilt at
the end of the seventeenth, and this view of it, engraved for the *Gentleman's
Magazine* in 1812, shows a casual concession to classic architecture, in the
form of supporting columns, Doric and Tuscan, though the general character
of the building is Jacobean.

fragraunte floures in their bedchambers and privy roomes, with
comfortable smell cheered mee up and entirelye delyghted all
my sences."[1]

Although classic architecture was as little understood in the
sixteenth century as industrial design in the nineteenth, the
Elizabethans had what the Victorians conspicuously lacked—a
sense of style. Their tall, carved chimney pieces, inexpertly

[1] *The Touchstone of Complexions*. Generallye appliable, expedient and profitable for
all such as be desirous and carefull of theyr bodyly health . . . First wrytten in Latine
by Levine Lemnie, and now Englished by Thomas Newton. (London: 1581.) Quoted
by William Brenchley Rye in *England as Seen by Foreigners in the Days of Elizabeth
and James I*. (London: John Russell Smith, 1865.) Pages 78–9.

adorned with oddments of antique ornament, and the bulbous legs of their tables and the columns supporting the tiers of their court cupboards, crowned with rudimentary Ionic capitals, might seem clumsy and ill-proportioned, but the rooms in which they appeared had an air of vitality, derived partly from the opulence of the decoration and the virile structural lines of the furniture, but largely from the confident, unashamed enjoyment of rich surroundings that distinguished their owners, who had mastered the art of living, and tempered their exuberant enjoyment of life with an innate respect for common sense (see plates 6 and 7).

3

ARCHITECTURAL ENLIGHTENMENT
AND PURITAN AUSTERITY

URING the first half of the seventeenth century the significance of the classic orders of architecture as controlling elements in design was gradually apprehended. Sir Henry Wotton's paraphrase of Vitruvius, entitled *The Elements of Architecture*, was published in 1624, in which he described the characteristics of the orders "according to their dignity and perfection," and by giving to Tuscan, Doric, Ionic, Corinthian, and Composite a human likeness, introduced an agreeably informal method of discoursing upon a technical subject. "The Tuscan," he wrote, "is a plain, massie rural Pillar, resembling some sturdy well-limb'd Labourer, homely clad. . . ." It was "of all the rudest Pillar, and his Principal Character *Simplicity*."[1] The Doric was "the gravest that had been received into civil use, preserving, in comparasion of those that follow, a more *Masculine Aspect* and a little trimmer than the Tuscan that went before, save a sober garnishment now and then of *Lions heads* in the *Cornice*, and of *Tryglyphs* and *Metopes* always in the *Frize*. . . The *Ionique Order* doth represent a kind of Feminine slenderness, yet saith *Vitruvius*, not like a light House-wife, but in decent dressing, hath much of the *Matron*. . . The *Corinthian*, is a *Columne* lasciviously decked like a Curtesan, and therein much participating (as all Inventions do) of the place where they were first born: *Corinth* having been (without controversie) one of the wantonest Towns in the world. . . . The last is the Compounded *Order*: His *name* being a brief of his *nature*. For this Pillar is nothing in effect, but a *medly*, or an *amasse* of all the precedent *Ornaments*, making a

---

[1] *The Elements of Architecture*, by Sir Henry Wotton. First published, 1624, and included in *Reliquiae Wottonianae*, with Izaak Walton's *Life*, issued in 1651. The third edition is quoted (1672), Part I, page 23.

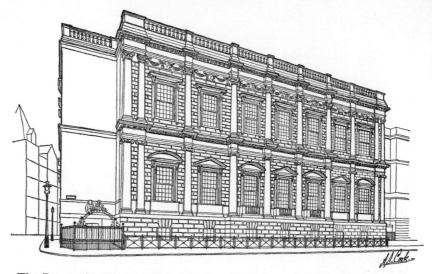

The Banqueting House, Whitehall, London (1619–1621), designed by Inigo Jones, the first great English architect to use the classic orders as a system of design and not as ornamental adjuncts to a façade. His buildings, as Stanley C. Ramsey has observed, "were not merely Italian transcripts, but as English as the stone of which they were built." The influence of his work educated the taste of the Jacobean aristocracy, and gradually refined and unified the work of craftsmen—masons, joiners, carvers and smiths. *Drawn by A. S. Cook.*

new kind, by stealth; and though the most richly tricked yet the poorest in this, that he is a borrower of all his Beauty. . ."[1]

The opening sentences of Wotton's work set forth the beliefs that had inspired all good builders and other craftsmen in England for centuries. "In *Architecture*, as in all other *Operative* Arts the *End* must direct the *Operation*," he said. "The *End* is to build well. *Well-building* hath three Conditions, *Commodity*, *Firmness*, and *Delight*."[2] A few pages later in his essay he touched, perhaps unconsciously, on the conflict and confusion that still bedevilled design, when he wrote: "*In Architecture* there may seem to be two opposite affections, *Uniformity* and *Variety*, which yet will very well suffer a good reconcilement, as we may see in the great Pattern of Nature . . ."[3]

[1] Wotton, *opus cit.*, Part I, pages 24–5.
[2] *Ibid.*, page 6.   [3] *Ibid.*, page 16.

These "two opposite affections" were reconciled by craftsmen as the Elizabethan period merged into the Jacobean, when taste was informed by the architectural settings which Inigo Jones (1573–1652) designed for the court masques, and later by his buildings. The influence of that first great English practitioner of classic architecture gradually refined and unified the work of craftsmen. When he began his career as an architect, England had many unbroken links with pre-Reformation civilisation; men were still living who remembered the glories of the great religious houses before they were despoiled; the ideal of United Christendom still inspired Europe and as yet there was no thought of severance with the past, no reference to "The Middle Ages"—a phrase coined later in the seventeenth century by the German scholar, Christoph Keller.[1] So it was neither revolutionary nor remarkable that the submerged English tradition in design should break through once more to the surface of life during the middle years of that century, reasserting its characteristics with fresh strength and inventiveness. This was not a revival of an old style; it was a restatement of native gifts, creatively expressed in the crafts, particularly those connected with building, and it was the prelude to national understanding and acceptance of the classic orders and all that they implied as a universal system of design. Before that wide understanding was established, England passed through the shadows of the Puritan period, which affected the character of design by pruning the extravagant growth of opulent decoration, particularly on furniture. Luxurious display of any kind invited the suspicion of grim and godly fanatics and, as in modern totalitarian states, suspicion was usually followed by persecution.

Unable to endure the repressive policy of the Puritan government, many English gentlemen who valued privacy and independence travelled in Europe, so one result of Cromwell's dictatorship was to liberate craftsmen, temporarily, from another—the dictatorship of fashion. During this respite from foreign and modish influences much of the confidence they had lost in the previous century was restored. Tools and methods of producing and fabricating materials were gradually improved in many crafts and industries, and the work of joiners, carvers and turners

[1] Christoph Cellarius (1638–1707), whose proper name was Keller.

was invigorated, although some casualties occurred in luxury trades. Fine crystal, for example, was condemned as a survival of royalist extravagance: wine-glasses were for tipplers, mirrors pandered to vanity: art was basically sinful, and as for pleasures, William Prynne had pointed out in his *Histriomastix* that they were "no part, no particle of a Christian's comfort; he can live a most happy joyful life without them; yea, he can hardly live happily or safely with them."

Despite the dismal climate of the age, the ancient human love of ornament survived and was satisfied without ostentation largely through the skill of carvers and turners. In 1633 the formal separation between the work of joiners and turners was laid down by the Court of Aldermen, and thereafter the two branches of woodworking were segregated: no turner was allowed to work in a joiner's shop, and all turned work had to be sent out. The severity of furniture design during the Puritan period was modified by the ingenuity of turners and carvers. Hitherto, decorative effects had depended largely upon the carver who cut flutes or gadroons on turned work, or used gouge carving on flat surfaces; but the turner became inventively independent, and instead of producing spindles, balusters and bulbs for subsequent enrichment by another craftsman, gave initial decorative character to such turned members as chair and table legs and stretchers by using combinations of knob and ball, ring and bobbin, and introducing the twist or spiral cut, with variations. The carver used architectural motifs with greater discretion during and after the Jacobean period, such as arcaded panels, which appeared on the fronts of chests, bed heads, chair backs, chimney pieces and walls. (See pages 21, 23 and 24.)

During the Commonwealth, in audacious defiance of the enveloping gloom, a note of gaiety, indicative of latent high spirits, could be detected in the work of the joiners, carvers and turners, who in collaboration improved the technique of furniture design and introduced or extended the use of such conveniences as the gate-leg table, chair table, and that forerunner of the chest of drawers, the mule chest. Oak, hitherto the chief material for joinery and furniture making, was now frequently supplemented by various fruit woods, like apple and cherry, also by ash, elm and yew, while walnut was occasionally used, sometimes for such

An early Georgian terrace of four houses on Richmond Green, Surrey, known as Maids of Honour Row, as they were built in 1724 to house the Maids of Honour attending the Princess of Wales. In the windows of the ground and first floors four panes are used in each sash, though the slenderness of the glazing bars suggests that the original sashes may have been replaced later in the eighteenth century. The storeys are marked horizontally by white string courses, and the top storey has a series of recessed brick panels which carry up the lines of the windows above the cornice, so the vertical elements in the elevation are not abruptly terminated. *Drawn by A. S. Cook.*

members as the supporting columns on a court cupboard, though base and tiers would be of oak. Throughout the country a growing capacity for mechanical invention was in evidence among craftsmen. Evelyn describes a door lock "that for its filing and rare contrivances was a masterpiece, yet made by a country blacksmith. But, we have seen watches made by another with as much curiosity as the best of that profession can brag of; and, not many years after, there was nothing more frequent than all sorts of iron-work more exquisitely wrought and polished than in any part of Europe, so as a door-lock of a tolerable price was esteemed a curiosity even among foreign princes."[1] He also mentioned a forerunner of the mechanism used in a taximeter, shown to him by Colonel Blount, which was "the application of the *way-wiser* to a coach, exactly measuring the miles, and showing them by an index as we went on. It had three circles, one pointing to the

[1] *Diary*, July 16th, 1654.

number of rods, another to the miles, by 10 to 1000, with all the subdivisions of quarters; very pretty and useful."[1] In 1631, Charles I granted a charter to the Clockmakers Company of London, and the great age of English clockmaking began. A spirit of scientific enquiry was stirring, stimulated by ingenious inventions, like those produced by Cornelius Drebbel, the Dutchman who settled in London, enjoyed the patronage of James I and Charles I, and invented among other things, an effective method of refrigeration, a submarine vessel that could be rowed and navigated under water, a glass which gave sevenfold reflections, and a perpetual motion device. Such engineering projects as the draining of the Norfolk and Lincolnshire Fens, begun in mediaeval times, were undertaken. The first sketchy outlines of the industrial revolution were discernible, though so far power was produced only by water or wind, springs or weights, and the operation of gravity. The cast iron industry became established, and began to expand after 1650, although many royalist ironworks in the Weald and the Forest of Dean were demolished as a result of the Civil War.

Many members of the nobility and gentry came back from their self-imposed exile when they realised that the Puritan government was firmly in the saddle, and they brought with them fresh ideas. Evelyn returned from Paris with a pattern for his first coach.[2] The pages of his diary are thronged with new notions, and disclose how the educated, wealthy man of the period regarded design. Perhaps his most illuminating statement about contemporary taste was made during his visit to Rome in 1644, where he saw the Palace Farnezi, that was built, as he put it, "when Architecture was but newly recovered from the Gothic barbarity."[3] This is an echo of the fashionable intolerance for all forms other than classical, that characterised taste in the previous century, but with this difference: Evelyn, and thousands of other gentlemen, knew that classic design represented order and lucidity while their fathers and grandfathers had thought of it merely as the modish "Italianate" way of building and decorating. This new enlightenment ultimately ended the conflict between craftsmen and fashionable designers; for during the second half of the seventeenth century craftsmen began to understand what the fashionable

---

[1] *Diary*, August 6th, 1657.   [2] *Ibid.*, April 29th, 1652.
[3] *Ibid.*, November 4th, 1644.

In many English inns, two or three centuries of building, each with their characteristic methods and materials, are associated in one structure, incorporating brick, plaster, weather-boarding, open galleries, the casements of the Tudor and Jacobean periods and the orderly sash windows of the Georgian age. The George Inn, Southwark. *Drawn by A. S. Cook.*

designer was attempting to create, and the designer—who was
generally an architect—exercised a clarifying educative influence.
Old ideas and prejudices remained, but in time a full and practical
understanding of the freedoms and possibilities inherent in the
classic orders of architecture spread through the country. This
fresh understanding first affected builders, masons and joiners;
then woodworkers generally, and metalworkers.

The man whose example had fostered and made possible this
national comprehension of the significance of the great system of
design had died, in 1652, disappointed and thwarted, without
ever seeing the results of his work; but it was to that man, Inigo
Jones, that the subsequent Golden Age of English design owed its
strength and universal acceptance.

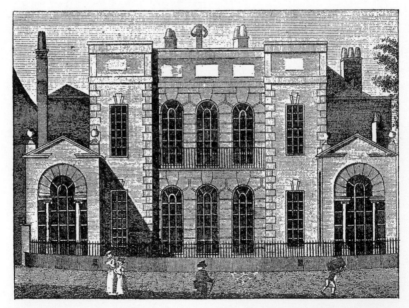

The windows dominated the façade of the Georgian house, whether it appeared
in a village or in some fashionable London street or square, or was built at
the beginning, middle, or end of period. Great country mansions might have
porticoes, ascending through two or more storeys, but the windows and
their proportions were always an integral and vital part of the design. This
view of Lord Cathcart's House in Whitehall was published in the *European
Magazine*, February, 1797.

The unifying element in Georgian architecture, apart from the use of classic mouldings and ornament, was the double-hung sash window, which replaced the casements of the sixteenth and seventeenth centuries. Part of Bedford Street, Woburn, Bedfordshire, showing the Black Horse Inn and adjoining shops. *Drawn by Marcelle Barton.*

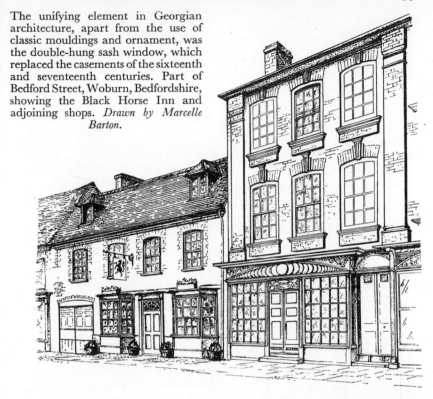

When Charles II returned to England, the music and the shouting that greeted him certainly heralded something much more important than the restoration of that cheerfully astute and lascivious monarch. The rejoicings were sincere, for the restoration closed a bleak period of austerity, of urgent exhortation, and constant prying into the large and small matters of life, and the English revelled in their new freedom from interference. With a king once again established in Whitehall, and those grim Puritan regional controllers, Cromwell's Major-Generals, either in flight, exile, or awaiting execution, England threw its hat in the air; and almost immediately a gay, spontaneous exuberance was apparent in the design of all kinds of things. Everywhere men with skill and ingenuity were at work, breathing again the air of freedom, without fanatical overseers

D

From the late seventeenth century to the 1830's, English towers for sacred and secular buildings were graceful and imaginative examples of the classic idiom of design. They arose in the cities and towns of England and the North American Colonies, where the influence of architects like Wren, Hawksmore, Gibbs and Chambers permeated. Many were light, airy structures, like this example, which shows the upper part of the tower of St. Anne's, Soho, designed by William Talman in 1714 and added to the church, which was built by Wren, 1680–1686. Wren's tower, which this replaced, is shown in Kip's view of London (1710). Talman's tower was rebuilt by S. P. Cockerell in 1802–1806, and this still remains, an odd, bulbous structure that survived when the interior of the church was destroyed by bombing in 1940–1941. Reproduced from a print by B. Cole, 1754.

glowering their disapproval: goldsmiths and silversmiths, weavers and clockmakers, cabinet-makers and chair-makers, joiners, carvers, turners and glass-makers; and, controlling all the activities of such people with intelligence and highly civilised standards of taste, were accomplished architects. The golden age of design had begun; it lasted approximately one hundred and seventy years, from 1660 to 1830, and gave to the towns and cities and homes of England and the American Colonies a benign and unforgettable beauty. In England, despite the reckless destruction

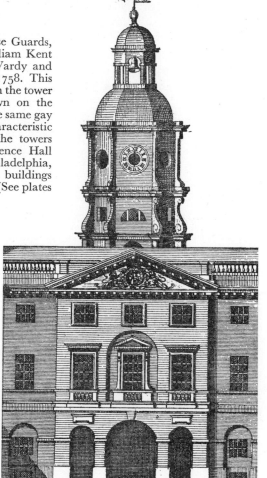

The East front of the Horse Guards, built to the designs of William Kent after his death, by John Vardy and William Robinson, 1750–1758. This is a more solid structure than the tower of St. Anne's, Soho, shown on the opposite page, but it has the same gay elegance—an agreeable characteristic that is also apparent in the towers and lanterns of Independence Hall and Carpenters' Hall, Philadelphia, and those on the restored buildings of Williamsburg, Virginia. (See plates 12 and 13.)

of the past hundred years, much of our architectural heritage remains; in the United States, apart from such enlightened examples of preservation and reconstruction as Williamsburg in Virginia, New England is rich in buildings, civic, sacred and domestic, that were derived from the work of Wren, Hawksmore, Gibbs and other architects of the late seventeenth and early eighteenth centuries. The College of William and Mary at Williamsburg, built in 1695–1698, is attributed to Wren (see plate 13). Regional interpretations of the English tradition in classical architecture and furniture design were developed in the American colonies, from New England in the north to Georgia in the south (see plates 12 and 13).

The chief achievement of the golden age was to bring into coherent relationship the design of everything that was made, through the universal comprehension and use of the rules of proportion. Gibbon, indulging his power of graceful compression, observed that "the practice of architecture is directed by a few general and even mechanical rules." It sounds like a facile over-simplification, but Gibbon's words reflect the urbane acceptance of those rules, which provided recognised standards for critical judgement. They were applicable to the making of nearly every-thing that was used by people in every walk of life; and because they were understood and their relative simplicity was explained in clearly written and well illustrated copy books, craftsmen were enlightened by them. There was none of the resentful muddling with proportions and ornamentation that had occurred in the sixteenth century. Everything derived benefit from the discerning study of the orders of architecture; everything acquired gracious-ness of form while preserving that basic English characteristic, common sense, which demanded stability and good workmanship, thus preserving what Sir Albert Richardson has called "the controlling balance of tradition."[1] Even the arrangement of ornamental patterns printed or woven on fabrics, stamped on leather, painted on china, or engraved on metal, exhibited the influence of those "few general and mechanical rules" which gave such felicitous certitude to this new phase of English design.

The study of architecture was obligatory alike for men of taste, who were the patrons, and the designers and artist-craftsmen who worked for them. Within a century of the Restoration, Thomas Chippendale acknowledged the obligation in the first paragraph of his preface to *The Gentleman and Cabinet-Maker's Director* by saying: "Of all the Arts which are either improved or ornamented by Architecture, that of CABINET-MAKING is not only the more

[1] "Taste of the Eighteenth Century," by Sir Albert Richardson, PP.R.A., F.R.I.B.A., published in the Annual Report of the Wisbech Society, 1958.

The replacement of Gothic buildings by classic designs continued for over two centuries. *Right:* St. Mary's Church, Battersea, completed in 1777. *Drawn by A. S. Cook.* The original church is shown below. *From a contemporary print, circa 1750, in the author's possession.*

useful and ornamental, but capable of receiving as great assistance from it as any whatever. I have therefore prefixed to the following designs a short explanation of the five orders. Without an acquaintance with this science, and some knowledge of the rules of Perspective, the Cabinet-Maker cannot make the designs of his work intelligible, nor shew, in a little compass, the whole conduct and effect of the piece. These, therefore, ought to be carefully studied by every one who would excel in this branch, since they are the very soul and basis of his art."[1]

The architect was the master-designer, recognised and respected as such by his patrons, and by workers in every craft, whose activities were directly or indirectly influenced by the proportions and characteristic ornament of the classic orders.

[1] *The Gentleman and Cabinet-Maker's Director*, by Thomas Chippendale. (London: printed for the author and sold at his house in St. Martin's Lane. 1754.)

4

MASTER-DESIGNERS AND
ARTIST-CRAFTSMEN

ARLY in his reign, Charles II appointed as Assistant to the Surveyor General a young man named Christopher Wren, whom Evelyn had described as a "miracle of a youth" and a "prodigious young scholar," who at the time of this royal appointment was Savilian Professor of Astronomy at Oxford. A mathematician, an artist, and an amateur of architecture, Wren was identified with the new, innovating spirit of scientific speculation, and seven pages of Bishop Sprat's *History of the Royal Society* are devoted to an account of his inventions and experiments. The former included improvements to astronomical and optical instruments; the latter a method "of injecting liquors into the veins of animals," which originated the technique of blood transfusion.[1] Most gifted and famous of English architects, the designer of St. Paul's Cathedral was perfectly clear in his own mind about the significant responsibilities of his profession. "An architect," he said, "ought to be jealous of Novelties, in which Fancy blinds the Judgement; and to think his Judges, as well as those that are to live five Centuries after him, as those of his own Time. That which is commendable now for Novelty, will not be a new Invention to Posterity, when his Works are often imitated, and when it is unknown which was the Original; but the Glory of that which is good of itself is eternal." In another aphorism on design he said: "Architecture aims at Eternity; and therefore the only Thing uncapable of Modes and Fashions in its Principals the Orders."

The orders supplied a framework for fashions of every kind, gay, fantastic, engagingly absurd at times, but regulated and given

---

[1] *The History of the Royal Society*, by Thomas Sprat. (London: 1722, the third edition corrected.) Section XL, page 317.

Georgian decorative labels, of the kind used by confectioners and apothecaries: the influence of contemporary architecture is apparent in the ornament selected, particularly the urn. *From the author's collection.*

decorative coherence by the universal acceptance of the classical idiom. The golden age of design passed through its growing pains; but by the end of the seventeenth century they were over. As a natural reaction against Puritan repression, designers often indulged in profuse displays of ornament, but such light-hearted essays in extravagance were wholly different from the rather

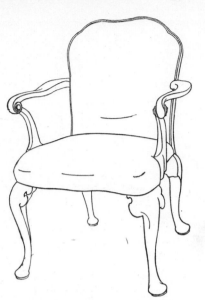

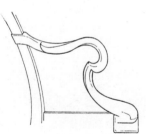

The new curvilinear conception of chair design in the early eighteenth century made a complete break with the stiff, upright lines of the Puritan and Carolean types, which still had obvious affinities with the box-like chairs of the early sixteenth century. (See plates 4 and 10.) *Above left:* An early Georgian elbow chair with a "bended back," scroll-over arms, cabriole legs and claw-and-ball feet. *Above right:* An elbow chair of the same period with a stuffed seat and back. The graceful curves of a scroll-over arm are shown on the left. *Drawn by Marcelle Barton.*

ponderous work of the late Elizabethan and Jacobean periods. Carolean chairs and day-beds and cabinet stands might be expansively florid with carving and gilding, but such things were never clumsy, they never had the corpulent solidity of form, cherished by under-educated taste, which seldom knows how to begin or where to stop with ornament. New materials and new techniques came into use when the cabinet-maker's craft was introduced. Walnut was used for furniture, and presently mahogany.

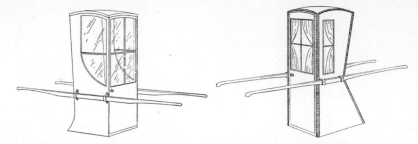

Two sedan chairs of the type used in Bath in the late eighteenth and early nineteenth centuries. A memory of the form of the sedan chair was preserved by the body of the hansom cab. *Drawn by Marcelle Barton.*

Directly the classical system of design was understood and practised throughout the country, designers were able to deal with craftsmen who worked in an accepted idiom, so when things were designed and made all the parties concerned spoke the same language. Designers and craftsmen were united in partnership: very often the craftsman was the master-designer, perhaps the head and directing genius of a family of craftsmen. When Evelyn recorded the launching of the *Charles* at Deptford, he said that "she was built by old Shish, a plain honest carpenter, master-builder of this dock, but one who can give very little account of his art by discourse, and is hardly capable of reading, yet of great ability in his calling. The family have been ship-carpenters in this yard above 100 years."[1]

The pattern of modern industrial production was occasionally anticipated by the working methods of architects like Wren, Vanbrugh and Kent, and organisers of skilled labour, such as Thomas Chippendale. The allocation and distribution of tasks in a building or a workshop by master-designers and artist-craftsmen had more in common with organised work in a mid-twentieth-century factory than with the collective skill of mediaeval craftsmen, working in a flexible partnership. The benefits of the system outweighed any disadvantages: it was not repressive and gave ample opportunity to imaginative craftsmen to breathe new life into ancient forms. Foreign ideas were absorbed and happily anglicised. The irresponsible froth of rococo fashions, the successive

[1] *Diary*, March 3rd, 1668.

waves of oriental taste, the mournful sobriety of Gothic motifs, were all gracefully accommodated. English patrons might lose their hearts to a foreign mode, but designers never lost their heads. To rococo fashions, they said, in effect: "You can be amusing without being loose!" Curves were always under control, as the chair-makers of the Queen Anne and Early Georgian periods proved by their new curvilinear conception of chair design, which melted away the last traces of Puritan stiffness without diminishing the robust quality of their work. Chairs afford one example of a fresh understanding of the structural and aesthetic significance of complementary curves. There were many others. (See page 47.)

The ubiquitous influence of the classic orders fostered national appreciation of good proportion and determined the nature and placing of ornament. The lanterns of a ship; the carved figurehead on the bows; the gilded metal lamps of a coach; the shape and decoration of a sedan chair; the carved and gilded or crystal chandeliers that hung from the ceilings of fashionable drawing-rooms, the sconces on the walls, the silver candlesticks on the nobleman's dining table or the brass candlesticks in the cottage, all bore the impress not only of a universal system of design, but

A private coach, standing outside the premises of Hatchett, the coach maker in Long Acre. An elegant combination of plate glass and painted and varnished woodwork. From a contemporary print, published in 1783.

Escutcheon and knocker, executed in brass water gilt, for the outer door of 20, St. James's Square, built for Sir Watkin Williams-Wynne, 1772–1774, to the design of Robert Adam. Reproduced from *The Works in Architecture of Robert and James Adam*, Vol. I, No. IV, plate VIII, 1773. Classical motifs are used with precision and restraint. Such firm, orderly composition was the antithesis of rococo —even the relative sober anglicised versions, like the example shown below, from the third edition of Chippendale's *Director*, plate CC.

Design for a chandelier, from plate CLIV of Chippendale's *Director*, third
edition, to be executed in wood, gilded and burnished.

of a common approach to every problem of design. The operation
of the system was disclosed by excellent proportions and the
confident use of ornament; the common approach was apparent
in the way materials were selected and used. The carved decoration
on the stern gallery of a man-of-war; the scrollwork on the hilt
of her captain's sword; the chasing on the silver mounting of his
pistols and the case and works of his watch; the shape and embellishment of the silver on his table at home, the salt cellars, sugar

The rococo style originated in France, and grew with exuberant gaiety during the early part of the Louis XV period, and affected English taste during the middle years of the eighteenth century. In the hands of English carvers and cabinet-makers it became less extravagant, though the French style had a beneficial effect on English furniture design by modifying the stiffness and slimming away the corpulence that had characterised early Georgian woodwork. In this girandole by Chippendale French influence is apparent, but the ruined Gothic column with the broken arches springing from it reflects the prevailing taste for mediaeval oddments. From the third edition of Chippendale's *Director*, plate CLXXVII.

A pier glass frame, another
example of English rococo,
from the third edition of
Chippendale's *Director* (plate
CLXXIV). This acknowledges
the Chinese taste, as the girandole on the opposite page acknowledges the Gothic: both
examples have a firm, robust
framework for the gay and
fanciful carved ornament. (See
pages 50 and 51.)

castors, cream jug and teapot, the decanters and glasses on his sideboard, all his furniture, and, outside his house, the brass door knocker, the mud scrapers, the gates, lamps, and railings, the character of the street where he lived and the coach in which his wife went visiting, all bore witness to a great release of educated inventiveness; recognisibly classical in origin, and yet as English as beef and beer, or oak and ash and thorn.

The robust quality of English design was never inimical to elegance. For example, the lettering and cursive script used on clock faces and barometers, on the silver wine labels suspended on decanters or set out in gold on the glass (see plates 20 and 27), on apothecaries' bottles and pill boxes, on tradesmen's cards, signs and notices, on tombs and monuments and on the title pages of books and magazines, exhibited a classical perfection of form and execution.

Writing masters, like John Baskerville (1706–1775) of Birmingham, who became famous printers, designed clear and elegant types. (This book is printed in the typeface he invented, which is named after him.) Nearly all the capital letter forms were derived from the incised inscriptions on the monuments of ancient Rome, and rich, precise, variously decorative but always legible

Right: A pier glass and table, designed as a decorative unit, with the slender lines and delicate classic ornament characteristic of the work of the brothers Adam. *Below:* A side table with pedestals and urns, which, like the house opposite, shows the elegance designers like Robert Adam achieved in the handling of classical motifs. *Drawn by Ronald Escott.*

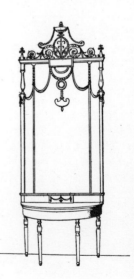

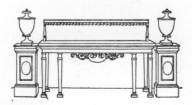

No. 7, Adam Street, Adelphi, London, by Robert Adam, *circa* 1770. The Greek anthemion ornament has been used as a motif on pilasters, frieze and balcony railings. *Drawn by David Owen.*

versions of those basic models were devised by English signwriters, engravers and typefounders.

Not only were designers confident, and executant craftsmen competent and informed: patronage was educated. The easy accommodation of foreign ideas had become almost a national habit, like the easy hospitality England gave to refugees. Tyranny and persecution in Europe periodically enriched England with brains and skill, as the oppressive conservatism of the Old World was later to enrich North America with enterprising and adventurous settlers. In many crafts and industries patterns and devices that had evolved originally in China or ancient Greece, were transmuted into something characteristically English. The variety of English accomplishments in design during the golden age was

E

astonishing. Silversmiths produced some of their finest work in the Georgian period; at Braintree and Spitalfields silk weaving flourished; china and pottery had grown from small country crafts into vast industries and the wares of Chelsea, Fulham, Worcester, Derby and Bow became famous. Most progressive and inventive of all pottery businesses was Wedgwoods, with its new works at Etruria near Hanley in Staffordshire. Josiah Wedgwood's epitaph states that he "converted a rude and inconsiderable Manufactory into an elegant Art and an important part of National Commerce." His influence on the design and technique of English pottery was comparable to the influence of Inigo Jones upon English architecture. He greatly improved domestic ware, and "he supplemented the use of the primitive potter's wheel by afterwards turning his ware upon an improved lathe. He was the actual inventor of at least twenty new bodies for the manufacture of earthenware. . . ."[1]

Gay colours, delicate or bold patterns, sensible and graceful shapes, were characteristic of the work of the great English potteries, though the delicacy never became faded or finicky, or the boldness too brutally vigorous. There was occasionally a rustic jollity about some of the patterns and scenes that adorned mugs, plates and jugs; and the English landscape, incomparably lovely in its gentle and continuous variety, was a favourite subject; but it was Wedgwood who popularised classical motives. He was one of the first industrialists to grasp the significance of industrial design and established a practical system of collaboration with artists and sculptors. It was successful, but the example of that partnership between art and industry had little or no effect upon later generations, either in the pottery industry or others, and it was not revived until the present century.

Wedgwood lived and worked and organised the production of his wares during the time when the First Industrial Revolution was already beginning. Unanticipated, unrecognised, with its colossal powers for good and evil as yet unsuspected, that revolution destroyed the English tradition in design in many industries, and produced a new rich class, far more ignorant and tasteless than any new rich class had ever been before. The tidy, compact world of the eighteenth century, in which good design was the

[1] *A Catalogue of the Wedgwood Museum, Etruria*, by Frederick Rathbone, "Biographical Notes," page 16.

The double-bowed shop front of Fribourg and Treyer's, the tobacconists,
34, Haymarket, London; a late eighteenth-century example which illustrates
the prevailing mode for slender glazing bars in windows and the use of delicately
moulded detail. *Drawn by A. S. Cook.*

rule and nearly everything men made or used gave satisfaction and delight to the eye, gradually disintegrated, and a few generations later the traditions, the habits of thought and the knowledge which characterised the golden age of design were lost, its achievements denigrated, while craftsmen and skilled technicians were afflicted and thwarted by a new age of confusion, as their ancestors had been three hundred years earlier.

5

VICTORIAN CONFUSION AND
INDUSTRIAL DESIGN

EVER since the rise of a new rich class in the early nineteenth century, taste in England has been partly conditioned by the intimidating need for "keeping up with the Joneses," irrespective of whether the Joneses were worth keeping up with or not. Taste arising from envy is a poor stimulant for creative design; taste arising from admiration is a very different social and artistic force; while both forms are abhorrent to rebels and pioneers, who, with the insolent confidence of genius desire to make everything new, or whose disapproval of contemporary life inspires a sentimental though sincere regard for the distant past. During the eighteenth century taste at the top was worth imitating, for, as Dr Johnson observed: "When the original is well chosen, and judiciously copied, the imitator often arrives at excellence which he could never have attained without direction; for few are formed with abilities to discover new possibilities of excellence, and to distinguish themselves by means never tried before."

The faultless taste of the aristocracy, the abundant common sense of executant craftsmen, and the widespread understanding of the rules governing the proportions of the classic orders of architecture, gave everybody in Georgian England standards of judgement, sharpened their critical abilities, and brightened their visual powers. Keeping up with cultivated and modish noblemen and gentlemen was far less enervating to national taste than keeping up with members of a barbaric plutocracy, wholly destitute of any sense of style, who knew what they liked, possessed the money that allowed them to indulge their whims, but lacked the artistic perception which would have made the things of their choice worth imitating. After the 1820's, they also lacked the expert guidance of conscientious and well-informed tradesmen,

Windsor is the name generally used for chairs and seats of stick construction. The Windsor chair is one of the few articles that survived the transition from manufacture by individual craftsmen to mechanical production. *Above:* examples of comb-back chairs with cabriole legs, mid-eighteenth and early nineteenth century.

Above: Two hoop-back chairs, with spur stretchers, mid-eighteenth and early nineteenth century. (See opposite page for later developments of the type.) Windsor chairs were manufactured extensively in the English North American colonies during the eighteenth century, with regional variations of design, and the comb-back type was generally preferred. (See plate 37.)

Left: A form of Windsor chair known as a Smoker's Bow, first made during the second quarter of the nineteenth century. The name was probably derived from the bow-shaped back and the widespread use of the type in smoking rooms and inn parlours. *Right:* A variation of the Windsor type, known as a Mendlesham or Dan Day chair, said to have been originated in the early nineteenth century by Daniel Day of Mendlesham and Stoneham in Suffolk.

who could follow Sheraton's advice when he wrote in *The Cabinet Dictionary* that "In furnishing a good house for a person of rank, it requires some taste and judgement, that each apartment may have such pieces as is most agreeable to the appropriate use of the room. And particular regard is to be paid to the quality of those who order a house to be furnished, when such order is left to the judgement of the upholsterers; and when any gentleman is so vain and ambitious as to order the furnishing of his house in a style superior to his fortune and rank, it will be prudent in an upholsterer, by some gentle hints, to direct his choice to a more moderate plan."[1]

Such "gentle hints" would have been ill-received by a purse-proud mill-owner who wanted to advertise his prosperity with lavish display and who probably disapproved of the morals and manners of the nobility and gentry, thus unhappily uniting vulgarity and puritanism. It was regrettable that the growth of

[1] *The Cabinet Dictionary*, by Thomas Sheraton. (London: 1803.) Entry FURNISH, pages 215–16.

a morally earnest and largely uneducated rich class coincided with the development of mechanised industry in the early nineteenth century, and we are still suffering from the devastation caused by this disastrous concurrence of social change and industrial progress, for we have inherited a legacy of oppressive ugliness. The mechanical production of furniture, for example, was from its early days dedicated to cheap, slick imitations of hand-made models; though one of the early propagandists for industrial design, John Claudius Loudon (1783–1843), included some prophetic suggestions in his vast *Encyclopaedia of Cottage, Farm, and Villa Architecture and Furniture* (1833). Chairs of wood and metal are shown in those crowded pages, some of them designed, at the age of twenty-two, by Robert Mallet (1810–1881), the famous civil engineer, who built Fastnet Rock Lighthouse. They are odd, clumsy forerunners of the tubular metal furniture of the 1920's, bearing about the same relationship to such work as Neanderthal man bears to Homo sapiens. (Loudon had a flair for discovering and encouraging young men of talent: he published Ruskin's first essay, written at the age of fifteen, in his *Magazine of Natural History*.) Mallet's designs were for chairs with cast iron frames, and wooden seats, supported on tubular legs. In the 1830's and 40's many experiments were made with metal furniture, particularly with rocking chairs, but the most characteristic Victorian design employing contemporary materials was the metal bedstead, that satisfied both the love of ornament and the obligation to be up to date. The Victorians also desired comfort: not entirely in the deeply upholstered sense, but through the cosy abundance of their furnishing and the variety and richness of their possessions. The industrial revolution accelerated the debasement of design; the eyes of the English died some time between 1830 and 1880, and only slowly and painfully did the nation partly recover its sight. It is still more than half blind.

The new and promising materials and techniques for handling them, introduced by the First Industrial Revolution, were misused: the machine was seldom allowed to do its splendid best; mechanical production was largely employed to simulate articles and patterns formerly made by hand, and cheapness and quantity dominated the ideas of industrialists. To produce goods cheaply in abundance was excellent; they were designed badly, not

The Cabinet-Maker's shop, 1830. Reproduced from the frontispiece of the fifth edition of *The Cabinet-Maker's Guide, or Rules and Instructions in the art of varnishing, dying, staining, japanning, polishing, lackering and beautifying Wood, Ivory, Tortoiseshell, and Metal*, by G. A. Siddons. In the Introduction, the author observed that his was perhaps "the only work that may properly be called a Manual of the Arts, and the rapid sale which it met with, is a proof of the estimation in which it was held . . ."

because bad design lowered their price, but because it was thought necessary to make them "look rich," which gave machine-made things a vulgar reputation. The term "cheap and nasty" became familiar, while "machine-made" was a term of abuse. Such labels retarded the development of industrial design, although the English genius for design and the English tradition were unconsciously expressed in new activities. Some of the great engineers of the nineteenth century were unrecognised industrial designers of a high order, and such things as locomotives and the appliances and architecture of railways, the signal cabins, some of the stations, the great bridges and viaducts, followed the English tradition in design. (See plates 32, 33 and 34.) When engineers tried to be "artistic" they usually defaced their work.

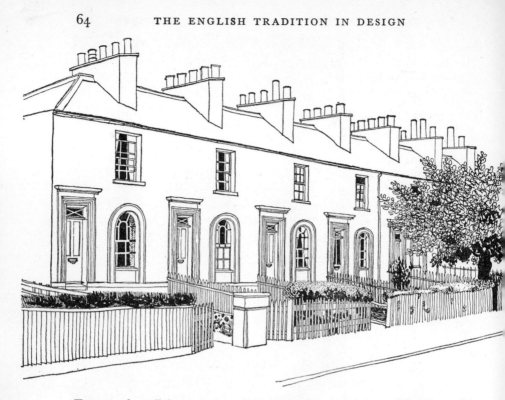

Terrace of small houses, *circa* 1835, in the Lower Richmond Road on the north side of Mortlake Green. Classical mouldings are used for the architraves of the front doors and the arched windows on the ground floor. Georgian grace in buildings and the design of street furniture, railings, lamps, the early letter boxes and such things as drinking fountains survived far into the nineteenth century. (See plate 35.) *Drawn by David Owen.*

The Great Exhibition of 1851 was housed in a building that was a triumph of industrial design and gave a preview of the New Western Architecture that was to develop during the next hundred years. Joseph Paxton (1801–1865), one of the great though unacknowledged industrial designers of the time, had created the first large-scale prefabricated building of wrought and cast iron and glass, but was quite unaware of the magnitude of his achievement, and never, apparently, suspected that he had invented a new technique that was to have a profound effect upon architectural design. Neither did anybody else, and Ruskin asserted his disbelief in the future of glass and iron in building. It was unlikely, he said, that they would "ever become important elements in architectural effort," and supported his statement by referring to the Bible, where he did "not find that iron building is ever alluded to as likely to become *familiar* to the minds of men; but, on the contrary, that an architecture of carved stone is continually employed as a source of the most important illustrations."

Nearly every English exhibit in the Crystal Palace showed that as the Victorians had mistaken "comfort for civilisation," they had also mistaken ornament for design. Those responsible for making things, thought chiefly of "applying art," of spreading over surfaces some form of decoration, copied without understanding from some mediaeval or classical prototype.

Many influences had combined to produce this new age of confusion, but the mischief was done by the Romantic movement, encouraged by the novels of Sir Walter Scott with their amiably misleading pictures of the Middle Ages, and by the Gothic Revival, which had changed an elegantly fantastic Georgian fashion into a symbol of Christian respectability. John Ruskin preached artistic salvation through Gothic forms, denouncing with passion the classical system of design and the Georgian age that had used it with such lucidity and grace. The architect ceased to be the master-designer, becoming instead a style fancier, a copyist and an adapter of the various periods of Gothic architecture. The "Battle of the Styles," classic versus Gothic, distracted the architectural profession, while the sense of style was lost, and the rise of the new industrial architecture and the emergence of industrial design were unobserved. Henry John Randall has said that "The Gothic revival, especially in the nineteenth century, was one in which the perfection of the mechanism failed to conceal the departure of the spirit."[1] Ruskin honestly believed that a return to Gothic forms would free designers from the restraints which the classic orders had imposed, would liberate fresh ideas, and inspire great art. But the Gothic Revival often encouraged limp imitation and led to lavish mixtures of all kinds of ornament, so that mediaeval, Renaissance, and naturalistic motifs in

[1] *The Creative Centuries*, by Henry John Randall. (London: Longmans, Green & Co., 1944.) Chapter 27, page 191.

ambiguous association darkened the design of all kinds of things, fireplaces, sideboards, cruets, lamps, clock cases, garden seats—everything, in fact, except the new industrial and railway architecture.

People with plenty of money to spend, the new rich and the increasingly prosperous middle classes, were enchanted with all the complexities of form that arose from this rich confusion of ideas; it was the best of all possible worlds. Certainly it was a great age of literature, of enterprise, of exploration, like that earlier age of confusion, the first Elizabethan; but there was no appreciation of form and colour, no capacity for judging whether an article was well or ill proportioned; the ineluctible darkness that only the blind know and endure had descended; but with this difference—the Victorians had no idea that they had lost their sight.

6

THE HANDICRAFT REVIVAL

IN 1861 a firm of decorators was founded, called Morris, Marshall and Faulkner, inspired by the idea of producing and selling things that would be well made, properly designed and agreeable to live with. This company was formed by a group of men, led by William Morris (1834–1896), the son of a prosperous broker, who after leaving Oxford had studied architecture as a pupil in the office of George Edmund Street. The other members of the company included Dante Gabriel Rossetti, Edward Burne-Jones, Philip Webb, Maddox Brown, Faulkner and Marshall. Today, Morris would be called an escapist; but he was really a revolutionary reformer, whose ideas of revolution went into reverse. He loathed the lush complacency of his own age, disliked the messy squalor of industry, realised that machinery was being used the wrong way and often for the wrong ends, and felt with the profound sincerity of which great creative minds are capable, that the only hope for England and her skilled and patient people was to restore respect for well-made things by reviving the crafts which were dying out, and bringing back to the lives of craftsmen and workers generally the joy and pride and sense of personal fulfilment in labour which had been, if not wholly destroyed, severely diminished by the First Industrial Revolution.

Like Sir Walter Scott, Morris idealised the Middle Ages, though William Cobbett's denunciatory *History of the Protestant Reformation* was his inspiration rather than Scott's genteel mixture of tinsel and chivalry; so with an ingenuous disregard of realities, he imagined mediaeval England to be a paradise of joyful work, of singing, happy craftsmen, the home of a great band of Christian brothers, carving stone and wood, painting and gilding, hammering metal into fantastic shapes and colouring glass, all for the glory of God and the crafts. He wanted to live in that sort of

67

England himself and described in *News from Nowhere* just the sort of society he desired to create. His gentlemanly socialism, like the gentlemanly taste for Gothic in the previous century, had a gracious quality; his work had honesty of purpose and unforced gaiety, which brought a new breath of life to design in England. Some of it may have been self-conscious and artificial, just like some of the people with whom he associated, those mid-Victorian highbrows who thought mediaeval art was a nice hobby to have; but he did restore much of the respect for skilled work that had been lost in the England that had confused ornament with design. He reminded his countrymen that the executant craftsman could also be a designer, instead of a helpless, willing tool; he believed that the designer should also be an executant craftsman. He detested the dictatorial technique of the man at the drawing board, believing that the man who worked at the bench generally knew more and should not be subservient to a mere fanciful draughtsman. Morris perceived that designers, who were in his day seldom more than men with untrained imaginations whose solitary accomplishment was drawing, had lost their old knowledge of materials; they were widely separated from the craftsmen and mechanics who executed or manifolded their ideas; and he realised that love and understanding of materials was the wellspring of English skill. He set about mastering a variety of crafts himself and threw into this work a prodigious versatility, that enabled him to design and make fabrics, to dye his own materials for weaving, to carve and decorate woodwork, to design type-faces, to set type and print books, and to make things in metal. His influence grew, and one conspicuous result of it was the founding of the Art Workers' Guild in 1884; another was the encouragement his example gave to a new type of artist-craftsman, who was not a skilled interpreter of current fashions, like the great cabinet-makers of the Georgian period, but a man who wanted to practise the arts and to turn his creative gifts to the mastery of some craft or group of crafts, by developing small industries on a craft basis. These isolated activities, separated from contemporary economic and industrial life, were at first only the palest reflections of the light that blazed from Morris's own work and writings and speeches; but the artist-craftsmen gradually became established. Throughout the countryside they settled down to work in wood and metal, to weave and to make pottery, and gradually they found patrons. Though they were ignored by industry, they began to have an impact on taste and, although quite unaware of performing such a function, they occasionally initiated research work in design from which organised industry ultimately though unconsciously derived benefit.

William Morris and those who helped him to revive handicrafts certainly opened the eyes of their fellow countrymen; but the effect of the Romantic movement and the First Industrial Revolution was still too strong for the English to see clearly. They were without critical standards. They respected the new enthusiasms for good workmanship; they liked to think of "hand-made" things, but the results were not gratifying to Morris, nor did they resurrect the English tradition in design. As a master-craftsman, he had during thirty years or so, edited for his contemporaries the ideas of an England so old, so out of tune with the turbulent enterprise and seemingly boundless prosperity of Victorian England, that he had, unintentionally, fostered a new respect for old things, based upon the romance of age and not upon merit of design. Industry soon catered for this new form of taste; metal-work was produced, mechanically speckled with little dents to imitate hammer marks; woodwork was left with roughened surfaces; "hand-made" became a sales label; and as people began to collect antiques, genuine and spurious, the dealer came into his own.

The supply of antique furniture, china, pottery and metalwork, was abundant in the late nineteenth century; many graceful and elegant articles had been relegated to lumber rooms and attics to make way for the Gothic preferences of Ruskin's disciples or for richly ornamented and obviously comfortable things; but when the supply began to run short a new occupation for craftsmen was discovered—their skill was used for copying antiques and faking the evidence of age. No tyranny of fashion imposed by Renaissance or Jacobean noblemen, no limiting or destruction of skill by machine-production, had forced the wise hands of English crafts-men to act with such dishonour and futility. That debased industry was the worst by-product of Morris's great influence; it preserved an appearance of the English tradition, but was as lifeless as the embalmed corpse at an ancient Egyptian feast.

The work of the artist-craftsmen who were originally inspired by Morris, enjoyed a splendid vitality. It was partly through their individual skill that some lost threads of the English tradition in design were picked up. Perhaps the most outstanding was Ernest Gimson (1864–1919), whose genius found expression in cabinet-making, metalwork, embroidery, modelled plaster and book-binding. Men like Gimson and Sidney Barnsley, with whom for a time he was in partnership, did not pick up the threads of the English tradition from the point where they had been severed in the 1830's. They ignored the golden age of design, forgot everything that had happened between 1660 and 1830, and began where the mid-seventeenth-century English craftsmen had left off, thus recapturing, without antiquarian research or servile imitation, the spirit of the native English style, because they shared with the craftsmen of Puritan and pre-Renaissance England the same approach to the problem of using tools and materials and adjusting means to ends. There was nothing arrogant in their failure to acknowledge the existence of the great architects and cabinet-makers and potters and silversmiths of the eighteenth century, though it was a typically Ruskinian attitude of mind to regard those highly civilised men of genius as interlopers who had betrayed the English tradition and enslaved the crafts.

Between them, Ruskin and Morris in their vastly different ways, did much to confuse and muddle the whole subject of industrial design and to delay its identification as a characteristic manifestation of the machine age that was susceptible to study and creative direction. But the revival of the crafts in the latter part of the nineteenth century at least re-established an appreciative though limited understanding of pre-Renaissance English design, and initiated developments in cabinet-making, pottery, and the weaving and printing of textiles, that eventually affected industrial design.

7

THE RISE OF INDUSTRIAL DESIGN

ECAUSE of the insistence of Morris and the craft revivalists upon the basic importance of making things by hand, attention was deflected from the possibility of designing things properly for mechanical production. With few exceptions factory-made consumable goods had until the end of the nineteenth century been imitative, following some hand-made prototype, and arriving at an attenuated or blurred version of it. In the making of things for everyday use, the English tradition in design had been arrested, or rather kept in a state of suspended animation, though, like a feeble ghost, barely discernible, it still haunted the drawing offices of many industrial firms. Industrialists employed draughtsmen and regarded them as designers: usually they were men who could wield a pencil and copy a pattern, occasionally exhibiting a flash of daring by inventing some inept variation of a familiar form of ornament. The industrial designer, the man who could bring to the study of industrial processes and materials the sort of sympathetic comprehension that the executant craftsman gave to wood and metal and the methods for working them, had not yet been identified as a technician. Such men existed, but their work was not carried to a completed stage—it was not conceived as one problem, to be solved by trained imagination in association with technical knowledge; therefore the special aptitudes of many skilled men were thwarted and the work they often began so well was masked in its final stages by hack draughtsmen who applied the artistic trimmings.

It was impossible to re-establish the traditional gift of sympathy with materials while industrialists believed that it was "artistic" to imitate old patterns and disguise industrial materials. The more tolerant and discerning followers of Morris were aware that there was nothing intrinsically repellent in the nature of such materials.

"The easy contempt we feel for iron is the direct result of our unworthy treatment of it," wrote William Richard Lethaby on the subject of "Cast Iron and its Treatment."[1] Twenty-three years later Lethaby was admitting that "Although a machine-made thing can never be a work of art in the proper sense, there is no reason why it should not be good in a secondary order—shapely, smooth, strong, well fitting, useful; in fact, like a machine itself. Machine work should show quite frankly that it is the child of the machine; it is the pretence and subterfuge of most machine-made things which make them disgusting."[2]

Such reflections indicated the growth of a receptive mood on the part of critics and writers; a constructive change from the contemptuous indifference to everything connected with machine production which had accompanied the first rapturous enthusiasms of the craft revival in the 1860's and 70's. But the re-emergence of the English tradition through industrial production was long delayed; and at the opening of the present century ideas about the form and colour of all kinds of products were confused still further by the spread of a flamboyant foreign fashion whose irresponsible virility alarmed all but the boldest and most eccentric of the modish. Known in England as "New Art," it scrawled floreated devices over every surface with restless urgency, poured its writhing tendrils into innumerable moulds in foundries, while its practitioners inserted slips of brilliant enamel and bands of copper into woodwork and diligently cut heart-shaped apertures in cupboard doors and chair backs. It soon outwore its welcome by sheer anarchic turbulence; but it provided industry with a new label, and for a few years the shops were filled with modified and flimsy variations of those fluid Continental forms which fashionable taste had so swiftly discarded.

"New Art" was for a time regarded as "modern design" and seriously discredited the word "modern" as it was later discredited by the word "futurist." People played for safety and demanded old shapes and decoration so the antique dealers' prosperity was refreshed by a new enthusiasm among consumers, and the imitation of antique patterns was stimulated by the supposed failure of "modern" design. Industrial design was still

---

[1] *Journal of the Society of Arts*, February 14th, 1890.
[2] "Art and Workmanship," by W. R. Lethaby. *The Imprint*, January, 1913.

"The easy contempt we feel for iron is the direct result of our unworthy treatment of it," said Lethaby in 1890, writing on *Cast Iron and its Treatment*. But in the hands of a skilled designer cast iron became the most appropriate material for all kinds of mass-produced articles, large or small. Sir Giles Gilbert Scott, PP.R.I.B.A., chose it for the G.P.O. public telephone call boxes, of which thousands were cast and used throughout the United Kingdom. *Drawn from a photograph and reproduced by courtesy of the Postmaster General.*

undiscovered, though all the time it was making unperceived contributions to the English tradition, and a new machine art was arising, appreciated, apart from engineers, only by observant children and a few exceptional adults: for those people, using their eyes as men had used them a century earlier to appraise the form of ships and coaches and houses and furniture, saw beauty in the trim, untroubled lines of the locomotives that ran on the old Great Northern, London and North Western, and Great Western railways, and in the shapely hulls and superstructure of such neat and commodious vessels as the Birkenhead and Wallasey ferry boats that foamed back and forth across the Mersey. (See page 74.)

There were other directions in which the English tradition in design found unsuspected continuity; for example, in the early pillar-boxes, with their fluted sides and well proportioned domed tops, the public drinking fountains in London parks and commons, and the combined horse troughs and fountains (plates 34 and 35). Such things still showed the feeling for good proportion which designers and craftsmen enjoyed in the Georgian Age and invariably displayed, whether their work was cast in iron or carved in stone.

In 1937, James Maude Richards, one of the most penetrating and lucid critics of architecture, made a suggestive introductory

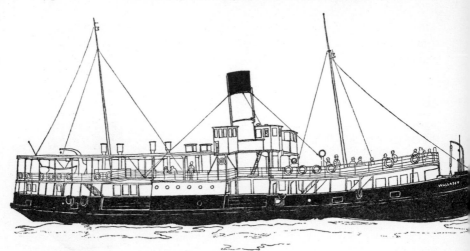

A Wallasey ferry boat, a type that has been in service ever since twin-screw vessels replaced paddle-wheel steamers early in the present century. (See page 73.) *Drawn by David Owen.*

study of characteristic forms of decoration and design, peculiar to England, in an article entitled "Black and White." He described as a national idiom of design "one that gets its architectural effect through the disposition of contrasted areas of black and white applied to the surface of an object." Its origin, he suggested, was almost certainly nautical, and he gave as typical examples, buoys, capstans, bathing huts, lighthouses and coastguard buildings. In concluding that the design of ships fostered this style, he observed that in the "pre-steam line-of-battleships, the black gun ports made a chequered pattern on the white hull." This treatment is found on many inns and cottages, and Richards recorded that "the lock machinery and other accessories of our canal systems are painted black and white; so are railway signals and other railway equipment. The railways have evolved out of cast iron a charac-teristic style of notices and signs; white letters raised in silhouette on a black background."[1] Signposts, Belisha beacons, traffic signals and direction signs were added to the list.

Such instances of continuity in the English tradition were seldom

[1] *The Architectural Review*, November, 1937. Page 166.

noticed or mentioned in the early years of the century. Between 1900 and 1914, there had been many hints that the native tradition in design was beginning to break through again; forcing its way back to contemporary life, not as a result of any conscious effort of resuscitation by industrialists, nor through any artificial craft revival, but because the national capacity for dealing with mechanical problems in a compact and orderly way was finding new outlets. That capacity, so vividly apparent in clock-making in the latter half of the seventeenth century, now inspired the design and production of such superb locomotive machines as the Rolls Royce. The idea that industrial design was a subject demanding intelligent study and attention, slowly gained acceptance. By 1914 it had achieved official recognition, for in that year a scheme was framed and sponsored jointly by the Board of Trade and the Board of Education for establishing a British Institute of Industrial Art, which was actually launched in 1920. Meanwhile, in 1915, the Design and Industries Association was formed, and its founders included men from industry and trade, like Frank Pick, Sir James Morton and Sir Frank Warner; designers, teachers and critics, like Sir Ambrose Heal, Harold Stabler, B. J. Fletcher and W. R. Lethaby. Industrial design had certainly been discovered though not clearly identified by a few far-sighted and exceptional people by the end of the First World War. Some of those enthusiastic discoverers of industrial design believed and persisted in believing that they had found the old joyful craft spirit humming away in the factory. Although they recognised the existence of industrial design, they were unable to apprehend that its genesis and nature were separate and apart from the craft revival, and habitually assumed that the work of artist-craftsmen like Ernest Gimson could be cited as exemplifying aesthetic excellence in the same breath as they praised the form of a well designed, mass-produced aluminium kettle or saucepan. The artist-craftsmen knew better: Gimson is quoted as saying: "Let machinery be honest . . . and make its own machine-buildings and its own machine-furniture; let it make its chairs and tables of stamped aluminium if it likes: why not?"[1] That was a plea for an honest acknowledgement of the respective virtues of design arising from the practice of handicrafts

[1] *Ernest Gimson: His Life and Work.* (London: Ernest Benn Ltd., Oxford: Basil Blackwell, 1924.) Page 14.

and the operation of industrial production; it echoed Lethaby's views in his essay on "Art and Workmanship." The products of industrial design had their own special excellence, "good in a secondary order," as Lethaby said, "shapely, smooth, strong, well fitting, useful; in fact, like a machine itself."

Another element in obscuring the real identity of industrial design, was the powerful reaction against the orgy of ornament, the overcrowding of rooms, and the obliteration of basic forms of furniture and nearly everything else that had persisted from the end of the Victorian period until the 1914–1918 war. This reaction led to a prolonged fast from ornament during the 1920's; a form of aesthetic abstinence that became confused with the reawakened interest in handicrafts and the wider recognition of the work of the great artist-craftsmen like Gimson. A new school of thought in architectural design confused the issue still further, for architecture, as always, was a basic influence in all branches of design and the intoxicating doctrines of M. Le Corbusier—whose books *Vers une Architecture* and *Urbanisme* appeared in English translation in 1927 and 1929—and the sober nourishment dispensed by Dr Walter Gropius from the Bauhaus at Dessau, gave some designers inspiration, others a kind of moral indigestion, which generated an almost pathological suspicion of ornament. A few desiccated intellectuals began to regard themselves as leaders of taste, though they avoided using the word *taste* as consistently as they abjured the terms *style* and *fashion*. Their putative leadership did not, in their view, depend on such transitory and ephemeral affairs as fashion, but upon an ability to think in a new and uninhibited way about design, for they belonged to the class of pioneer, mentioned earlier, that desires to make everything new. They were not so diversely qualified to fulfil the obligations of leadership as the cultivated nobility and gentry of the Georgian period, for they lacked the lusty love of life that has always distinguished periods of vitality in design and were as nervous of pleasure as the Puritans of the Commonwealth. So during the late 1920's and throughout the 30's good design was apt to be identified with abstinence from ornament, and unless designers were total abstainers they were likely to be written off by the *élite*, the *avant-garde* as they loved to call themselves, as traditional, reactionary, or *bourgeois*, a fearful accusation often made by those members of the *avant-garde* who were fuddling their minds with mixed political beverages. Functionalism raised its bleak head, and, with an air of triumphant revelation, old truths were rediscovered and loudly proclaimed.

To some extent the new puritanism in design was encouraged quite unwittingly, by the educational work of such bodies as the Design and Industries Association, which had helped to show up the ornamentally overburdened rubbish that had persisted after the First World War as a hang-over from the Victorian and Edwardian periods. The popularising of the slogan, "Fitness for Purpose and Pleasantness in Use," helped to restore respect for basic principles among designers and a few manufacturers; but by the mid-1930's that pure message had lost its air of brave, defiant innovation, for by then more and better architects and industrial designers were at work in Britain than there had been for some generations, and the English tradition re-emerged.

8

THE ENGLISH TRADITION IN
INDUSTRIAL DESIGN

DESPITE all the preliminary confusion that preceded the recognition of industrial design as a technical operation and the industrial designer as a neglected but indispensable technician, three aspects of the English tradition were apparent by the end of the 1920's. At the British Empire Exhibition, held in 1924, examples of every branch of industrial and decorative art were assembled and one of the most discerning and practical patrons of industrial design, Sir Lawrence Weaver (1876–1930) influenced the selection and display of the exhibits. It was easier after that exhibition had set new and higher standards—at least in the officially sponsored sections—to classify contemporary design broadly under three main sections:

I. The design of products in industries with a craft basis, such as printing, textiles, pottery, domestic glass and furniture.

II. Design in industries based almost wholly upon machine production, which manufactured such semi-mechanical articles as gramophones, refrigerators, cooking appliances of all kinds and, later, radio sets.

III. Industrial design for such large-scale mobile and static objects as railway rolling stock, trams, 'buses, trolley 'buses, motor cars, aircraft, railway station equipment, and so forth.

Those classifications are still valid. Sections I and II occasionally overlapped; for instance, some types of furniture were produced almost entirely by mechanical means, while some makers employed machinery only for converting material into workable units, thereafter using traditional tools and methods. Furniture by designers like Sir Ambrose Heal and Sir Gordon Russell, was never the result of a conscious compromise between hand-work and mechanical production; it derived benefit from all their personal research work in design, as practising and accomplished artist-craftsmen, and from their ability to organise and use mechanical methods where they were economically appropriate. Their furniture represented different but indubitable expressions of the English tradition.

Many outstanding examples of the emergence of that tradition in terms of large-scale industrial design were provided by the London Traffic Combine—that most enlightened precursor of the London Passenger Transport Board, which is now the London Transport Executive. The rolling stock, stations and equipment, signs, lettering and posters of the London Underground railways and the progressive development of vehicle design by the London General Omnibus Company, the Metropolitan Electric Tramways, and other constituent companies of the Combine, reflected in contemporary terms the English genius for the apt use of materials, the capacity to evolve tidy forms and employ gay finishes. Such triumphs of industrial design were made possible by the educated and enlightened patronage of Frank Pick (1878–1941), the joint managing director of the London Underground group and later the vice-chairman of the London Passenger Transport Board.

It may seem that all these various activities are unrelated and the expression of the English tradition in design is diffused and incoherent compared with the gracious unity of the golden age, when a universal system determined the designer's approach to every problem; but today there is greater scope than ever for the genius possessed by English designers for gaining sympathetic rather than dictatorial control over materials. Once again, woodwork affords a most instructive illustration of the perpetuation of that sympathy with materials, though now the decorative attributes of wood are differently accentuated. The furniture of such designers as Robert Wemyss Symonds (1889–1958), unlike the work of the Morris school of artist-craftsmen, continues the English tradition from the point where it was left by Thomas Sheraton in the early years of the nineteenth century. Closely akin to the spirit and character of our age, while recruiting some of its robust attributes from memories of the craft revival, is the sort of furniture designed by Sir Gordon Russell and his brother,

Professor R. D. Russell, who understand the technique of mechanical production. Architects like Christian Barman, Frederick Gibberd, Edward D. Mills, Sir Hugh and Lady Casson, Maxwell Fry, Jane Drew and Wells Coates (1895–1958), and industrial designers like Milner Grey, Misha Black and Ernest Race—to name only a few—have all accepted, studied and mastered industrial techniques. In common with the executant craftsmen of the Middle Ages, such designers exhibit intimate familiarity with materials, and they achieve and maintain a mastery of plywood and steel and light alloys, plastics and glass, as lightly and easily and untyrannically as the smiths, carpenters and masons of the thirteenth, fourteenth and fifteenth centuries who worked with iron and oak and stone. "Economy is a virtue proper to machinery," as Gordon Logie has observed in *Furniture from Machines*, "but there is a great difference between the economy that results from clean design and efficient production, and that produced by shoddy materials and scamped construction and finish."[1]

Things made from industrially produced materials tend to resemble machines in that they have everything to lose and nothing to gain from age. For example, "Machines used intelligently can produce furniture of excellent quality more cheaply than furniture made by hand. The furniture will not be the same as hand-made furniture. No machine can reproduce the delicacy and sensitivity of hand craftsmanship. What machines can do is to give us an altogether different kind of excellence."[2] But it is a transitory excellence: no machine-made article of furniture is likely to figure as an "antique" in a sale-room a century hence though it may be preserved in a museum as an object of historical interest in a world that has abandoned or outgrown industrial production.

Patronage has changed once again: it is no longer largely in the hands of an insensitive plutocracy, as it was in Victorian times, but is dispensed by various bodies, sometimes though not always as impersonal as machines, representing collective interests, or carrying out some official mandate. Large industrial corporations, nationalised industries, departments of the state

[1] *Furniture from Machines*, by Gordon Logie, A.R.I.B.A. (London: George Allen & Unwin, 1947.) Preface, page ix.
[2] Logie, *opus cit*.

like the Post Office and political or sectional organisations, like the Trade Unions, have all become patrons of architecture and industrial design. Many of the results of this new patronage are excellent, some pedestrian, a few deplorable. At least they have dispersed the apprehensions expressed over thirty years ago by Clive Bell, who was sceptical about the prospects of civilisation under democracy, because he had "not yet noticed that the soon-to-be-sovran proletariat, the working men of old England, manifest any burning desire to avail themselves of such means of civilisation as they already dispose of."[1] One of the most distinguished English examples of the new western architecture is the T.U.C. Building in Great Russell Street, London, designed by David du R. Aberdeen, F.R.I.B.A., and enriched with sculpture by Epstein.

Architecture, always the mistress art, has to a great extent determined the character of industrial design in the mid-twentieth century. The modern movement in architectural design, beginning in the early years of the century, was logical; but it has mellowed, like its practitioners, and is no longer coldly logical. It has a tenuous connection with science, and for a time was hampered by the sort of political affiliations that caused raving reactionaries like Hitler to stigmatise it as "the art of the left." No system of design has yet arisen from it, comparable with that based on the classic orders, but it has outgrown the grimness of uncompromising functionalism, which, as communism turns the milk of human kindness into hard, red cheese, tended to turn the joy of life into efficient living ("the house is a machine for living in," and all that). The impact of architecture upon industrial and domestic design, has been accompanied by a resurgence of interest in things made by hand, and there has been another formative influence in the character of what we now call "contemporary" design, namely the second Puritan period of the 1930's and 40's. This, like the previous Puritan period in the mid-seventeenth century, refined the form of things, censored luxurious trimmings and extravagances, the frills and agreeable follies that delight ordinary human beings (who are so much nicer than religious fanatics or godless intellectuals), and cleared the way for a glorious

[1] *Civilisation*, by Clive Bell. (London: Chatto & Windus. First published 1928. Phoenix Library edition, 1932, is quoted.) Section VII, page 255.

resurrection of colour and ornament and extravagance and zest for living, comparable with that of 1660.

The enforced austerity of the 1940's was hailed by some earnest reformers as a blessed opportunity for educating people about the virtues of plain and simple things, and those reformers were horrified when people who bought war-time utility furniture attempted to paint or carve its bare surfaces to make them seem more friendly. Some indeed would have liked to prohibit these innocent activities, but were restrained from advocating such an intolerable invasion of privacy by admitting that utility furniture was rationed furniture and was only there at all because we were engaged in the second great war of our century which was being fought to preserve the right of English people to do what they liked. But we have passed out of the Puritan period and are now confronted with the vague modishness of that label "contemporary," obviously impermanent, and, as it is being affixed to some very queer things indeed, decidedly ambiguous. If we called industrial design of the 1950's Neo-Elizabethan it would at least identify its period, which coincides in time with our emergence from austerity. But whatever it is called, design today is in a healthier and more virile condition than it has been for many years. More people are arguing and quarrelling about it, interesting themselves in it and abusing each other about its characteristics than at any time since the "Battle of the Styles." Everybody takes a hand in the controversy, from politicians upwards, and the views of educationalists, bureaucrats, industrialists, designers, and the common man—on whose behalf so many people speak, but, because he remains obstinately anonymous, never utters anything himself—are variously enlightening, prejudiced or absurd. There is ample evidence of a renaissance of imagination: the inhumanism of the 30's and the planned austerities of the 40's are almost forgotten. When this essay was first written, in 1946, they were still inhibiting the ideas of designers. Since then the Council of Industrial Design has been established, and has undertaken and is carrying through the immense task of educating industry and the public about design. War-time shortages and those that lingered on throughout the post-war period of reconstruction are over, and the designer has freedom to choose his materials, much as he wishes. There are far more industrial designers in practice now than there were in the 1940's: their own professional body, The Society of Industrial Artists, has improved their status by the most exacting methods of admission to the Society, so that industry may rely on the qualifications and competence of their members, as industry in the United States relies on the tested abilities of members of the American Society of Industrial Designers.

The Exhibition on the South Bank of the Thames, that most significant part of the Festival of Britain in 1951, was a form of stock-taking in national ability in design. It suggested, what has since become increasingly apparent, that we have largely out-grown the moral earnestness that infected all matters relating to design during the 1930's—so similar to the moral earnestness that inspired the Gothic Revival a century earlier—and designers may now be as gay and inventive as they desire. Many of them are, perhaps unconsciously, expressing national characteristics through their work, as surely and unmistakably as their forerunners in the seventeenth and eighteenth centuries. Thus the English tradition in design flourishes anew.

The threads of that tradition run back to mediaeval England, where they were first spun from the wisdom of men who worked with simple tools, few materials and abundant ingenuity. This brief sketch of a vast subject has indicated how those threads were unravelled in the sixteenth century, knitted up again into a great national pattern by the work of that master-designer, Inigo Jones, and once more unravelled when the golden age of design was destroyed by the First Industrial Revolution and the Romantic Movement in taste. William Morris and his followers attempted to pick up the threads once again, but only succeeded in weaving an archaic though lovely and instructive pattern, which they draped over the real problems of their age, and thus prevented the English tradition from finding conscious expression in terms of industrial design and production, until the third and fourth decades of our century. Before that happened the tradition was submerged by a wave of faking and imitation and the real English genius for design was masked by a false "Olde England"— a shoddy and flimsy form of taste which still persists. Only very slowly are patrons and consumers realising that "ye olde England" is neither old nor English but a shallow sham and that the real

English tradition in design is alight and alive all about us, in our homes and schools and public buildings, in our national interpretation of the new western architecture that has arisen from the now outmoded "modern movement," in the decorative shapes and patterns of domestic glass and pottery, in the gay and subtle patterns on textiles and wall-papers, in the design of public transport and the equipment and furnishing of ships and aircraft. In such work the spirit of English design resides: exuberant and vivid as ever, different in execution, but changeless in character.

THE PLATES

THE subjects of the forty plates have been selected and their captions written to illustrate as a connected story the manifestations of the English tradition in design from the Middle Ages to the present century. Many of them show how consistently architecture has influenced all branches of design. Contemporary examples have been deliberately confined to the last plate, which shows the impact of current architectural design on the form of furniture.

PLATE 1. Architecture is the basic visual art; its influence on many branches of design is apparent from the Middle Ages to the twentieth century. *Above:* Capital in the ruined nave of Buildwas Abbey, Shropshire, *circa* 1150. *Photograph by Daniel Nicholas. Below:* Valance on platform roof of Battle Station, Sussex. *Reproduced by courtesy of British Railways.* The scalloped decoration of the Norman capital and the fret of the Victorian valance are both examples of a simple, robust approach to design which characterises the English tradition.

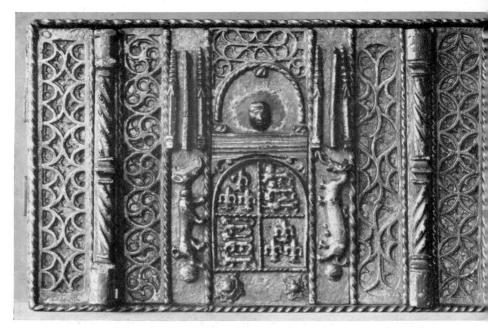

PLATE 2. Wrought iron lock, gilt, early sixteenth century, from Surrey.
The Royal arms and supporters are those of the house of Henry VII and
Henry VIII. The whole composition, as well as the various ornamental
devices, are inspired by the last phase of English Gothic architecture, the Perpendicular style. Compare this example with the far more elaborate steel lock
in the pierced brass case on plate 15. Both designs have derived their ornamental character from the architecture of their respective periods; both have
the same confident but respectful approach to the use of materials, which
enabled English craftmen, whether they worked in metal, stone or wood, to
be elaborate without becoming tortuous. *Reproduced by courtesy of the Victoria and
Albert Museum, Crown Copyright.*

Right: Escutcheon, *circa*
1480, Ryarsh Church, Kent.
From Parker's *Glossary*, Oxford, 1845.

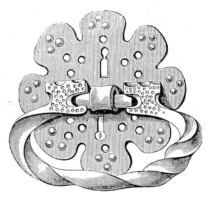

Aⁿ · DNI · 1571 ·
ÆTATIS · SVÆ ·
· 29 ·

Sir Richard Grenville, killed
in a sea-fight near the Azores,
1591

PLATE 3.   Portrait of Sir Richard Grenville, painted by an unknown artist in
1571. Helmet, body armour and the sheath of the sword below the hilt are
enriched with formalised acanthus leaves, far more clearly and confidently
delineated than those carved on the press cupboard on plate 7, and indicating
the armourer's understanding of the ornamental details of classic architecture.
Reproduced by courtesy of the Trustees of the National Portrait Gallery.

PLATE 4. *Left:* An oak joined chair, second quarter of the sixteenth century. *Reproduced by courtesy of the Victoria and Albert Museum, Crown Copyright.* The linenfold device, which was invented in the late fifteenth century, probably by Flemish craftsmen, appeared on four panels of the chair, and on the front and side panels of the early sixteenth-century chest below. The linenfold motif was originated by woodworkers; it had no architectural or classical prototype, and was used by European craftsmen with characteristic regional variations. The upper panel on the chair back is carved with Renaissance ornament.

PLATE 5. Sheldon tapestry panel, woven in coloured wools and silks, and silver gilt and silver thread, with the arms of Sacheverell as the central feature. (See pages 27 and 28.) Decorative hangings like this coloured the walls of rooms when the oak chair and chest on plate 4 were still warm gold in hue, before three centuries of polishing had enriched their tone. *Reproduced by courtesy of the Victoria and Albert Museum, Crown Copyright.*

PLATE 6. An oak draw-table, *circa* 1600, with bulbous legs and Ionic capitals above the gadrooning on the upper part of the bulbs. The acanthus leaves which decorate the main body of the bulbs are carved with delicate precision; but the Ionic capitals, like those on the press cupboard shown opposite, are crude, and suggest that the carver made a shot at an unfamiliar device and failed to bring it off, perhaps resenting the intrusion of ornamental forms that were still stigmatised as "Italianate." (See pages 16 and 30.) *Reproduced by courtesy of the Victoria and Albert Museum, Crown Copyright.*

Right: An example of the hybrid architecture of the late sixteenth and early seventeenth centuries. This porch is built on to Sunningwell Church, Berkshire, and has Gothic and classic features, with projecting Ionic columns at the angles, supporting an entablature. The doorway is a mixture of Gothic and classic details. John Jewel (1522–1571), Bishop of Salisbury, is supposed to be responsible for its erection. From Bloxam's *Principles of Gothic Ecclesiastical Architecture*, ninth edition, 1849.

PLATE 7. A press cupboard in oak, dated 1610, with heavily carved pilasters surmounted by Ionic capitals flanking the central arcaded motif. This motif is repeated on the sides. The lower part of the bulbous supports are carved with a rudimentary representation of the acanthus leaf. These oddments of ornament show, like the table on the previous plate, how little the significance of classic architecture was apprehended in the Elizabethan and Jacobean periods.

Reproduced by courtesy of the Victoria and Albert Museum, Crown Copyright.

PLATE 8. *Left:* Silver gilt standing salt and cover, bequeathed to the City of Norwich by Peter Reade, a mercer, in 1568, and made by Peter Peterson, a famous Norwich goldsmith. Height: 15¼ ins. Weight: 59 oz. *Reproduced by courtesy of the City of Norwich.* See page 22.

Above: Silver gilt rose-water ewer with salver (shown opposite), dated 1617. Height: 13¾ ins. Weight: 43 oz. 5 dwts.

PLATE 9. The Howard ewer and salver were presented to the City of Norwich in 1663, by Lord Henry Howard, who was created Earl of Norwich in 1677 and later in that year became the sixth Duke of Norfolk. The date letter is 1617, and these examples of Jacobean silversmith's work show a new mastery of classical ornament, particularly in the foliated scrollwork on the edge of the salver and the acanthus leaves encircling the raised medallion. The jocund, pagan sea-creatures disporting themselves both on the ewer and the salver contrast sharply with the subject depicted on the medallion on the salver, which is Christ washing the feet of the disciples. Diameter: $17\frac{3}{4}$ ins. Weight: 69 oz. *Reproduced by courtesy of the City of Norwich.* The ewer is shown on the plate opposite.

PLATE 10. A joined armchair of oak, *circa* 1630, with incised carving on the back panel, an arch enclosing a diamond. Very simple turning is used on the front legs and arm supports. The scrollwork on the cresting is derived from architectural motifs. *In the possession of Mrs Grace Lovat Fraser.*

Right: Turned and joined walnut chair, mid-seventeenth century. The turner was an independently inventive craftsman whose work did much to lighten the severity of furniture design during the Puritan period. *Reproduced by courtesy of the Victoria and Albert Museum, Crown Copyright.*

PLATE 11. Carved and turned walnut armchair, *circa* 1670, with cane-work in back and seat. The exuberant virility and freedom of the carved ornament celebrate the release from Puritan austerity. *Reproduced by courtesy of the Victoria and Albert Museum, Crown Copyright.* *Below:* A Charles II chest in veneered walnut. The decorative character depends largely on the use of oyster-wood veneering and cross-banding in sycamore on the edges of the panels, top, and drawer front. *From the collection of the late Robert Atkinson, F.R.I.B.A.*

PLATE 12. *Above, left:* The tower of Independence Hall, Philadelphia, Pennsylvania, designed by the Speaker of the Assembly, Andrew Hamilton (1676–1741). The foundations of Independence Hall were laid in 1731, and the building was completed in 1751. *Above, right:* The steeple of Christ Church, Philadelphia, designed partly by Dr. John Kearsley (1684–1772) and partly by Benjamin Franklin. The church was begun in 1727 and finished in 1754.

When the system of design represented by the classic orders of architecture was understood and imaginatively employed, buildings throughout England and the North American Colonies acquired new graces of form, while retaining the straightforward simplicity of the English tradition. This was apparent in the proportions of windows and doorways, in the composition of façades and the spacious elegance of the rooms within houses and public buildings, and especially in the gay variety of towers and steeples and lanterns. The lantern of Independence Hall, Philadelphia, and Talman's tower for St. Anne's, Soho, shown on page 40, are unmistakably English interpretations of classic architecture. *Photographs by the author.*

PLATE 13. *Above, left:* The Custom House, King's Lynn, Norfolk (1683), designed by Henry Bell (1653–1717), son of a Mayor of Lynn, and twice holder of that office himself. An example of the amateur in architectural design. *Above, right:* The College of William and Mary at Williamsburg, Virginia, attributed to Sir Christopher Wren, and begun in 1695. The present building is restored.

Above, left: Carpenters' Hall, Philadelphia, erected by the Carpenters' Company in 1770. *Above, right:* Restoration of the Governor's Palace, Williamsburg, Virginia: the original building was completed about 1720. *Photographs by the author.*

PLATE 14. Stern view of model of the *Royal William*, 1719. The impact of contemporary architectural design is apparent in the character and disposition of the ornamental details, the mouldings and pilasters. *Reproduced by permission of the Trustees of the National Maritime Museum, Greenwich.*

PLATE 15. Lock with case of pierced brass and blued steel, by Richard Pickford, London: second half of the seventeenth century. Like the wrought iron lock shown on plate 2, the composition and some of the ornamental motifs are inspired by contemporary architecture, and the locksmith's handling of a variety of devices with such orderly precision suggests a new mastery of decorative design. Formalised acanthus leaves and scrolls, grotesques, butterflies, cupids which might well be cherubs, and masks are elegantly disposed. *Reproduced by courtesy of the Victoria and Albert Museum, Crown Copyright.*

A bold, florid use of scrolls and classical motifs. A side table supporting a marble slab, designed by William Kent (*circa* 1685–1748). From *Some Designs by Mr. Inigo Jones and Mr. Wm. Kent,* published by John Vardy, 1744. (See page 41.)

PLATE 16. *Left:* English wineglass with a baluster stem, *circa* 1690. Height: 5¾ ins. diameter at rim, 2½ ins. at base, 2½ ins. Georgian elegance was foreshadowed during the last quarter of the seventeenth century.

Right: A Jacobite glass, *circa* 1720, engraved in diamond point with two verses of the Jacobite National Anthem and "Amen," inscribed in an arabesque medallion. Such specially engraved glasses were used by supporters of the exiled Stuarts to toast in secrecy the Young Pretender. Height: 6¾ ins. *Both examples reproduced by courtesy of the Corning Museum of Glass Corning, New York.*

PLATE 17. In architecture and the ancillary arts, England reached the highest level of civilisation in the Georgian period, though whether excellence in the design of practically everything used by people of all degrees may be accepted as a criterion has been, and is still, hotly debated. The faultless taste of the aristocracy was emulated by all classes, and the environment of the nobility and gentry, the rich merchants and professional men, doctors and lawyers, was immune from ugliness and vulgarity. William Hogarth, in his painting of "The Fountain Family," has depicted an outdoor scene, touched by the classical graciousness of the age. *From the McFadden Collection in the Philadelphia Museum of Art.*

H

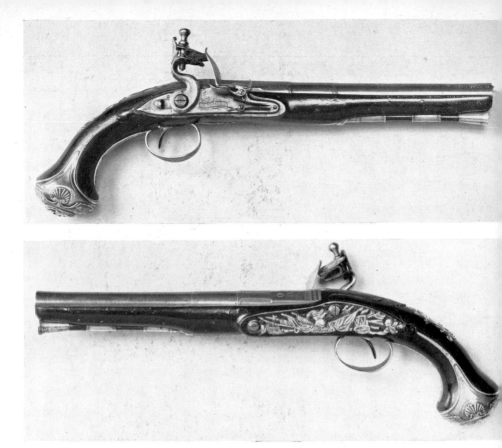

PLATE 18. A pair of flint-lock pistols with brass barrels. D. More, London, 1760. The universal acceptance of the classical idiom is apparent in the composition of the trophy on the side plate and the decoration of the butt. *Reproduced by courtesy of the Victoria and Albert Museum, Crown Copyright.*

Right: Trade card of Watts, the Bristol shot maker, *circa* 1780. *Reproduced by courtesy of the Trustees of the British Museum.*

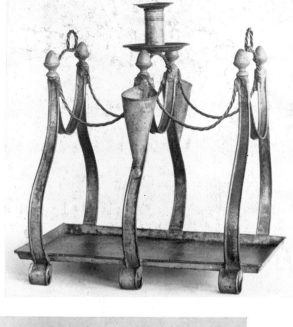

PLATE 19. *Right:* The finials on this tinned iron pipe-rack recall a form of acorn turning, and although the homely article was made in the mid-eighteenth century it has the characteristics of the pre-classical native tradition of design.

Above: A Sheffield Plate teapot of late eighteenth-century design. *Both subjects reproduced by courtesy of the Victoria and Albert Museum, Crown Copyright.*

PLATE 20. Silvered brass dial of a clock by John Godden of Wingham, in Kent, with rococo engraving in the centre. Small country clockmakers, in common with other rural craftsmen, followed the prevailing Chinese taste in their selection of ornament. The hood of this mahogany long-case clock has columns with widely-spaced flutes, brass capitals and bases and moulded detail derived from classic architecture. *Circa* 1775–80.

PLATE 21. Sign bracket from One Bell Inn, Thame. Late eighteenth century. An example of local smiths' work. *Reproduced by courtesy of the Victoria and Albert Museum, Crown Copyright.*

Left: Tradesmen's signs hung over the pavements of nearly every street before houses were numbered. A view of Fenchurch Street, London, in the mid-eighteenth century. From a contemporary engraving.

PLATE 22. *Left:* Corner cupboard in oak, the pilasters, frieze and drawer fronts veneered in mahogany, inlaid with thin lines of boxwood and ebony. Made in the countryside, at any time between 1760 and 1790, it relies for its decorative effect on the varied colours of materials. *In the possession of Mrs V. Atkins.*

Below: A mahogany chest, *circa* 1740–45, with carved cabriole legs and claw feet and one long drawer. *From the collection of the late Robert Atkinson, F.R.I.B.A.*

PLATE 23. Long-case clock in figured walnut, *circa* 1710–15. The treatment of the hood suggests the influence of contemporary architecture. The table is in Virginian walnut, a Queen Anne piece with a modified cabriole leg and hoof feet, lightly carved. The early Georgian mirror frame is of walnut and gilt gesso. *From the collection of the late Robert Atkinson, F.R.I.B.A.*

PLATE 24. *Left :* A Staffordshire jug of salt-glazed stoneware, 1765. The name "Thos. Allsop," enclosed in a wreath, appears on the front.

Right : Derby porcelain jug, about 1802. On the front are the letters "D.P.C." in cornflowers, the initials of Daniel Parker Coke of Trusley and Prixton (1746–1825.) *Both examples reproduced by courtesy of the Victoria and Albert Museum, Crown Copyright.*

PLATE 25. *Above:* Teapot, cream and coloured earthenware, Leeds or Staffordshire, about 1775. *Below:* Salt-glazed stoneware tea caddy. Staffordshire, about 1760. *Reproduced by courtesy of the Victoria and Albert Museum, Crown Copyright.*

Above: Silver-capped sugar castor, in deep blue cut glass, possibly Bristol, *circa* 1775. Total height with cap, $7\frac{1}{8}$ ins. *Reproduced by courtesy of the Corning Museum of Glass, Corning, New York.*

PLATE 26.   Spirit case in satinwood veneer, inlaid with other woods, with a hinged, slanting top. The interior is fitted with bottles and glasses. The arms and crest of the Adam family of East Hardwick, Yorkshire, are displayed on the bowed, central section. *Circa* 1793. The refinement of Georgian taste and manners are reflected in this gracious design. From *English Furniture in the Irwin Untermyer Collection*, Metropolitan Museum of Art, New York, 1958. Plate 327, Figure 376. *Reproduced by courtesy of The Hon. Judge Irwin Untermyer.*

PLATE 27. Coloured glass decanters, late eighteenth century. *Above left:* Deep blue. *Above right:* Green. *Right:* Glass ink bottle, *circa* 1850, and spirit container with dipper for lighting cigars. Both of these early Victorian examples show how Georgian elegance and simplicity of form persisted in the nineteenth century. *In the author's possession. Photographs by Sidney Newbery (above) and Reg Forster (right).*

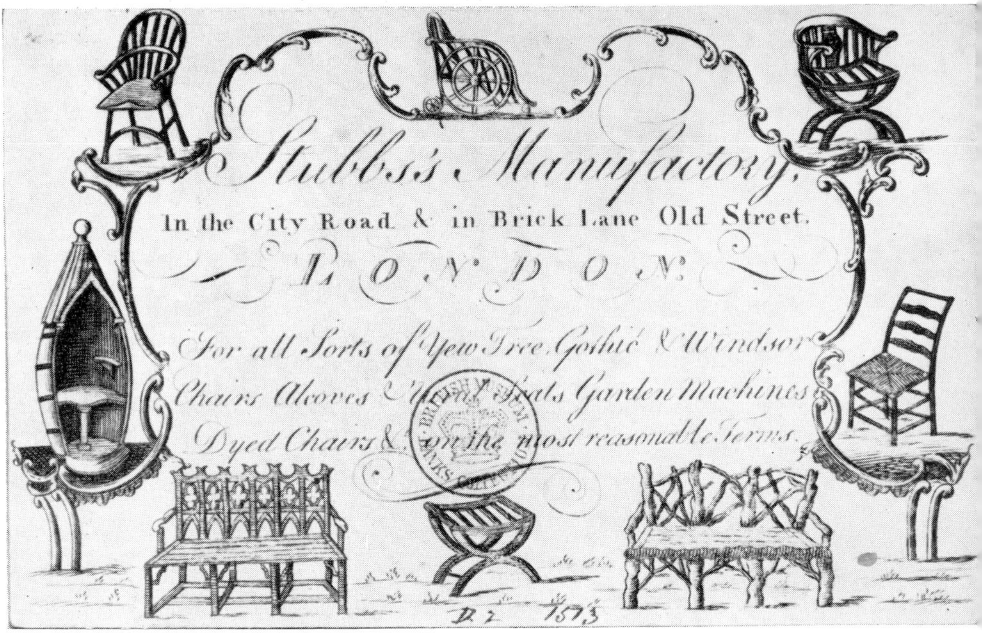

PLATE 28. The trade card of John Stubbs, 1790–1803, showing a range of furniture and a "garden machine," or wheeled chair. Rustic and Gothic designs are included. *Below:* Trade card of Strickland and Jenkins, cabinet makers, 1780–1793. The frame of classical design is free from the rococo flourishes of the Stubbs card. *Both examples reproduced by courtesy of the Trustees of the British Museum.*

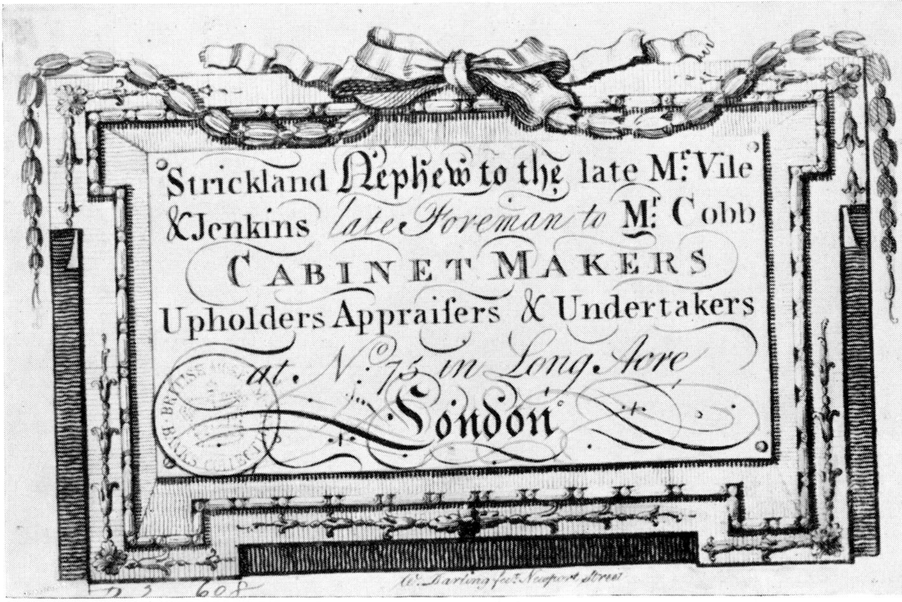

PLATE 29. Two early nineteenth-century perambulators, *circa* 1810. *Right:* A model in dark blue, with turned spindles. It has shafts and was probably drawn by a donkey or pony. *Below:* A barouche perambulator in yellow and dark green, with springs. *In the collection of Sir Albert Richardson, PP.R.A., F.R.I.B.A. Photographs by Sidney Newbery.*

PLATE 30. Early nineteenth century Wedgwood ware in slate grey.

Group of Regency objects: tea-caddy in rosewood: sewing-case in birdseye maple inlaid with ebony, brass and rosewood; and a silver christening mug, *circa* 1808.

PLATE 31. When George Morland painted this scene, entitled "Fruits of
Early Industry and Economy," industrial prosperity had not yet blunted the
sensibility of those engaged in commerce. Business men, like everybody else,
were still living in the golden age of good design, as every article in this room
attests—the octagonal cellaret, the decanter resting in a silver coaster, the
standish on the table, the wineglasses, the chairs, the picture frame, the
panelled walls and the slim section of the window glazing bars, all bear the
impress of classical taste. *From the McFadden Collection in the Philadelphia Museum
of Art.*

PLATE 32. Balance weight on the "Agenoria" locomotive, 1829: the lettering and the classical motifs and cable border are a conventional compromise
with an accepted idiom of design—as inappropriate as the top hats worn by
the driver and fireman of Stephenson's "Rocket." In the York Railway
Museum. *Reproduced by courtesy of British Railways. Below:* The "Rocket."
From *Our Iron Roads*, by Frederick S. Williams, 1852.

PLATE 33. Locomotive number plate, with bold lettering and numerals, emphatically legible in black and polished brass: one of those minor pieces of good design that passed unobserved in an age obsessed with dead styles and blind to the authentic industrial style that was arising wherever railways ran. In the York Railway Museum. *Reproduced by courtesy of British Railways.*

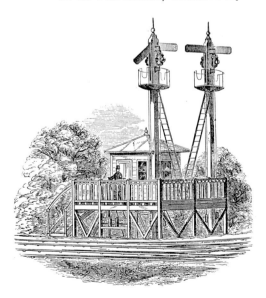

Left: An example of early railway architecture: signals and signal cabin. From *Our Iron Roads*, by Frederick S. Williams. (London, first edition, 1852.)

I

Plate 34. Cast iron railings on canal bridge in Wolverhampton, Staffordshire. This example of early nineteenth century design suggests the prevailing fashion for Gothic forms, and is admirably suited to the material. *Right:* An early cast iron fluted pillar box at Banbury, Oxfordshire. This preserves the classical tradition, though the moulded detail of the cap is rather heavy.

PLATE 35. The Victorian interpretation of the English tradition, uncomplicated by concessions to the Gothic revival. *Right:* Granite drinking fountain in Kensington Gardens, a standard design that was used in London parks and commons. *Below:* Horsetrough and drinking fountain, Roehampton Gate, Richmond Park. Late nineteenth century. *Photographs by Richard Grierson, A.R.I.B.A.*

PLATE 36. A three-ply woollen fabric, designed by William Morris for Kelmscott House, about 1879–80. Although the bird pattern dominates the design, the almost inevitable acanthus leaf intrudes, despite the designer's dislike of classical motifs. (See pages 69 and 70.) *Reproduced by courtesy of the Victoria and Albert Museum, Crown Copyright.*

PLATE 37. Country-made chairs.

Early nineteenth-century Windsor chair, with turned legs and
spur stretcher, in elm and yew.
(See page 60.)

Early nineteenth-century rush-
seated chair, a rural craftsman's
interpretation of a town fashion.

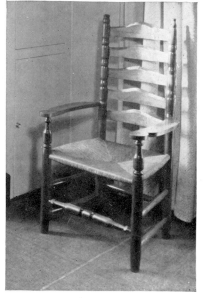

Ladder back rush-seated chair in
oak, designed and made by
Ernest Gimson

Ladder back rush-seated chair in
yew, designed and made by Sir Gordon Russell.

PLATE 38. Artist-craftsmen like Ernest Gimson (1864–1919) revived the spirit of the native English style, and were akin to the craftsmen of Puritan and pre-Renaissance England. They had nothing in common with the master cabinet makers and carvers of the Queen Anne and Georgian periods. (See page 70.)

Above: Cabinet in figured English walnut, designed by Ernest Gimson and made in his own workshop, about 1918. *Right:* Another example of Gimson's work: a bedside bookcase with drawers, in mahogany.

PLATE 39. *Right:* A dressing-table, toilet mirror, pair of candle-sticks and a stool of English walnut, designed by Sir Gordon Russell. *Below:* A sideboard designed in 1929 by Sir Ambrose Heal. Veneered walnut with a veneered sycamore interior. Both examples show how the English tradition in design was reinvigorated by the arts and crafts revival that William Morris initiated.

PLATE 40. The influence of contemporary architectural design on the form of furniture is clearly shown by these examples.

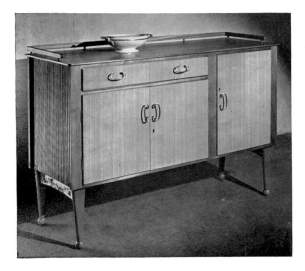

Above: The Sun House, Frognal Way Hampstead, London, by E. Maxwell Fry, F.R.I.B.A., *Drawn by Hilton Wright* and reproduced from *Guide to Western Architecture* by courtesy of George Allen and Unwin Ltd. *Left:* Sideboard designed by A. J. Milne for Heal & Son Ltd.

Below: Group of unit furniture, which may be arranged in various ways and supplemented by other pieces. Designed by R. C. Heritage for G. W. Evans Ltd. Reproduced from *Design in British Industry*, by courtesy of the author, Michael Farr.

INDEX

Page numbers in italics denote references in captions of illustrations in the text

K

GL